THE MYSTERY OF THE
TWO JESUS CHILDREN

By the same author:
Rudolf Steiner's Vision of Love
William Blake: Prophet of Universal Brotherhood
Michael and the Two-Horned Beast
Johannes' Pilgrimage in Rudolf Steiner's first Mystery Play
  (private printing)

THE MYSTERY OF THE TWO JESUS CHILDREN

and the Descent of the Spirit of the Sun

BERNARD NESFIELD-COOKSON

TEMPLE LODGE

For Ruth, with love and admiration.

Temple Lodge Publishing
Hillside House, The Square
Forest Row, RH18 5ES

www.templelodge.com

First published by Temple Lodge 2005

A catalogue record for this book is available from the British Library

ISBN 1 902636 65 1

Cover design by Andrew Morgan, featuring Bergognone's
'Twelve-year-old Jesus in the Temple'
Typeset by DP Photosetting, Aylesbury, Bucks.
Printed and bound by Cromwell Press Limited, Trowbridge, Wilts.

Contents

Acknowledgements

I wish to thank the Revd Malcolm Allsop for his encouragement and interest in this study of a complex and controversial subject. I also wish to thank Kit Gosset for his photographic assistance and Eileen Lloyd for her careful editing. My gratitude is also extended to Sevak Gulbekian of Temple Lodge Publishing for so willingly accepting this book for publication. As on earlier occasions I also express my gratitude to my wife, Ruth, for her understanding, patience and keen interest.

Plates

THE MYSTERY OF THE TWO JESUS CHILDREN

and the Descent of the Spirit of the Sun

In our endeavour to investigate the 'mystery' referred to in the title, we shall begin this introductory study[1] by first looking briefly at the genealogies of Jesus in the canonical Gospels of Matthew and Luke, and then proceed to consider the entirely different accounts of the infancy of the Jesus child as portrayed in these two Gospels. Consideration will also be given to accounts that have come down to us in New Testament apocryphal writings, in Aramaic and Hebrew documents discovered (1947 and 1952) in the Qumran caves west of the Dead Sea, and in writings by Syrian theologians of the thirteenth century. In particular, mention will be made of statements made by Rudolf Steiner, the Austrian philosopher, scientist and educationalist, who was the first in modern times to draw our attention to the reality of the existence of two Jesus children; consideration will also be given to his conception, expressed in different ways on a number of occasions, of the gradual descent of Christ, the Spirit of the Sun, from the spiritual world into a physical body. Reference will also be made to a few of the many works of art—largely by Italian artists of the Renaissance period—which illustrate some of the points raised in these pages.

*

The two different genealogies of Jesus, the Son of Mary, have been a baffling problem for theologians throughout the centuries. They agree that it is impossible to reconcile the two series of ancestors given by Matthew and Luke, let alone their stories of the birth of the child.

We notice that Luke traces the ancestry of Jesus right back

to Adam and, finally, to God the Father. Matthew, on the other hand, traces the ancestry of his Jesus child no further back than to Abraham. We then notice that the two genealogies are only compatible for 14 generations, that is, from Abraham to David, but then a split occurs. The Matthew genealogical tree goes from Solomon, the eldest, the royal son of King David; in Luke it goes from Nathan, the prophet-priest, another son of David. Matthew's genealogical tree contains all the kings of Judah. In addition to the 15 crowned kings of Judah, from David to Jechoniah,[2] the Matthew genealogy contains the royal motif by virtue of the three priest-kings[3] from the East and the fourth king, Herod the Great. After Nathan, the genealogy of Luke lists the names of unknown people, except, of course, those of Joseph and the child called Jesus.

That we are confronted here by two distinct genealogies and therefore also two different father figures both of whom were named Joseph—a name that was not a rarity—is borne out by the fact that the father of Joseph of the Solomon line is named Jacob, whereas the father of Joseph of the Nathan line is named Heli. That the mother of the Jesus child is named Mary in both genealogies need not surprise us. Mary was as common a name in those days as it is today. That the same name was given to the child in both genealogies need not surprise us either. It occurs also twice within that of Luke. In the 48th generation of the Nathan line we find the name Joshua, which is an earlier form of the name Jesus; both signify 'helper and bringer of salvation'.[4]

Here it is of interest to refer to a recent discovery. A French scholar, André Lemaire, claims to have found a 2000-year-old bone casket that may be the oldest physical evidence of the existence of Jesus. The stone chest carries an inscription in Aramaic which, translated, reads 'James, son of Joseph, brother of Jesus'. Lemaire dates the inscription to AD 63. He estimates that there could have been as many as 20 people called James in ancient Jerusalem (a city of possibly 40,000 residents at that time) with brothers named Jesus and fathers named Joseph.[5]

Now, there is no mention of brothers and sisters to the Jesus boy of Luke's Gospel. A disciple with the name of James is mentioned in his Gospel on three occasions, but not as being the brother of Jesus Christ. In Matthew's Gospel (13:55), on the other hand, we hear that Jesus had four brothers including one named James (see also Acts 1:14). Mark, in his Gospel, mentions the same four brothers and also two sisters (6:3). It seems justified to infer that the James mentioned in the Aramaic inscription could possibly refer to the brother of the Jesus of the Solomon line, but not, in short, to the Jesus of the Nathan line. This is borne out by a passage in one of the apocryphal Infancy Gospels, the *Book of James, or Protevangelium*, where we learn that Joseph was domiciled in Bethlehem, Judaea—the Joseph of Luke's Gospel lived in Nazareth, Galilee—and that he is a widower with sons, including, according to Matthew and Mark, one called James. In his Introduction to *The Festal Menaion*[6] Archimandrite Kallistos Ware of the Eastern Orthodox Church comments, '"Brother" is here understood by Orthodox to mean half-brother (perhaps child of Joseph by a previous marriage); or else cousin or other close relative.'

It seems paradoxical that both Matthew and Mark speak of Joseph of the Solomon line as being a carpenter; this does not appear to harmonize with the picture we have of the man to whose house in the City of David, Bethlehem, the three Magi came to worship the newborn child (Matthew 2:9–11). The stable is well suited to the Nazarene father and mother who come from a lineage of nameless 'quiet ones in the land',

and to the simple shepherds who came to adore the newborn child, so also is the work of a carpenter well suited to the Joseph we meet in Luke's Gospel. By contrast, the family we hear of in Matthew's Gospel descends from the most distinguished line of the nation. As Emil Bock reminds us, 'it is a family that we have to picture as a highly respected one of better social standing. The Joseph who Matthew refers to is of the "House of David". It is not without significance that the Joseph spoken of by Matthew lived in Bethlehem, the site whence descended his royal line.'[7] Jacobus de Voragine recounts that when Joseph 'had espoused the Virgin Mary, he returned into his city of Bethlehem for to ordain his meiny [i.e. retinue] and his house'.[8] Clearly then he was a man of some wealth. On their return from Egypt, however, instead of returning to Bethlehem the Solomon family took up residence in the rural community of Nazareth. Life there called for a number of adjustments on their part. In Bethlehem this family had enjoyed certain privileges due to education, wealth and social standing; in Nazareth, a close knit community, the Solomon family had to adjust to an ascetically simple lifestyle and relinquish the trappings of social privilege, if they were to live and work in harmony with the Nazarenes. We may then, perhaps, conjecture that the Solomon Joseph joined the Nathan Joseph in his carpenter's workshop, also that the educated and gifted Solomon Jesus boy would occasionally, or perhaps often, join the younger Nathan Jesus boy in the fields tending the sheep.[9]

*

The Christmas story of Matthew's Gospel is that of the learned and regal Magi; the story of Luke's Gospel is that of the humble, simple shepherds. Two completely different worlds are revealed to us. The appearance of the three Magi, three priest/kings,[10] with their retinues, not only aroused the ire of Herod the Great when he heard of the purpose of their quest but, we learn from Matthew, also 'troubled all Jerusalem with him' (Matthew 2:3).[11] Their visit to the newborn child was a very public event. Totally different was the world where the shepherds had their experiences on the night of the birth of the Jesus child. Shepherds were the simplest and humblest of people. They were hardly noticed by, even unknown to, those who dwelt in the town of Bethlehem. Their visit to Mary and Joseph and the holy child was a very intimate happening and certainly did not 'trouble' Jerusalem. The shepherds were as 'unknown' as the ancestors of Joseph who came after Nathan in Luke's genealogy, as unknown as the young, simple, innocent Mary whose home was the insignificant community, Nazareth. (See pp. 48–9 regarding Nazareth in the time of Jesus.) Luke allows us to recognize how through certain feelings of solemn devotion the soul is made receptive of supersensory, spiritual experiences. In the case of the country shepherds we hear that on a midwinter night, as they kept watch over their flock, 'the angel of the Lord came upon them and the glory of the Lord shone round about them [...] And they heard the joyous tidings that the Saviour had that night been born in Bethlehem.'

In relation to this experience, Emil Bock writes in *The Childhood of Jesus*:

> The radiant abundance of all the angelic hierarchies appears to the shepherds because the miracle and celebration of the winter solstice kindles the light of vision in their souls that have remained paradisal and childlike. [...] The hearts in Luke open to the light of spiritual experience like a bud that blossoms in the sun's light. This is the way of Mary [of Nazareth].[12]

Krüger gives us a glimpse of, a 'feel' for, the soul-quality of a shepherd of bygone days in the following vignette:

One of my mother's ancestors in the seventeenth century was a shepherd in a little village. I was always pleased to hear about him, and liked to imagine how for hours and hours the peaceable old man may have been standing at his resting-place, knitting socks in the shadow of an old lime tree, his wide earth-coloured cloak swirling around him in the wind, or in the midst of his 'Wollenherden'—i.e. woolly flocks—passing by the rough solitude of those hills, a friendly white-bearded patriarch, familiar to clouds and weather, also, maybe, with insights into the secrets of roots and herbs, a healer of wounds perhaps, anyway a taciturn simple herdsman with a warm sympathetic love for all fellow-creatures on earth.[13]

*

The mood of the Christmas story which has come down to us through the Gospel of Luke is completely different from that of Matthew. Whereas the former is one of simplicity, gentleness, peace, harmony and light, the latter is fraught with tension and tragedy, and overshadowed by darkness. Herod the Great's reaction to the news of the birth of the royal child stands in complete contrast to that of the Magi from the East. Whereas their hearts and minds are warmed by the knowledge of the birth of the Jesus child and filled with reverence, Herod is cold-hearted. The news of the birth of the 'King of the Jews' brought to him at his court by the three Magi gives rise to anger and fear in him. Out of deep-rooted megalomania and fear Herod commands that all children of 'two years old and under' should be slaughtered. In Luke we hear that the simple shepherds 'made known abroad' (i.e. to the few people they met that night in Bethlehem on the way back to their fields) the joyous news of the birth of the holy child; there is no mention of Herod. In Matthew the lamentations of the mothers of the brutally slaughtered infants ring throughout Bethlehem and beyond.

*

Before proceeding further with our consideration of the two nativity stories as given to us in the Gospels of Matthew and Luke we should note the following. Luke tells us that a decree was issued by the Emperor Augustus for a registration to be made throughout the Roman world and that Joseph went up to Judaea from the village of Nazareth in Galilee to register (enrol) at the city of David, called Bethlehem, and with him went Mary who was expecting a child.

Now, Ormond Edwards draws our attention to the fact that a Roman census could not have been carried out in Palestine during the time of King Herod the Great,[14] and draws the conclusion that both John the Baptist and the Nathan Jesus child could only have been born after his death.[15] Indeed, Herod the Great is not mentioned in Luke's Gospel. It is his son who is referred to in that Gospel, Herod Antipas (d. *c*. AD 40), tetrarch of Galilee and Peraea. He was responsible for the death of John the Baptist and was the ruler to whom Pontius Pilate sent Jesus Christ for questioning. (Luke 23:7–12.) Whereas, as we shall consider in due course, Matthew tells us that the Solomon Joseph flees to Egypt with Mary and the Jesus child to save the newborn boy from being killed by Herod the Great's soldiers, there is no such haste to leave Jerusalem in Luke's account. On the contrary, we hear that 'when the days of her purification according to the law of Moses were accomplished' (Luke 2:22), Mary and Joseph brought the Jesus child to Jerusalem, to present him to God.

We shall consider this presentation in the temple a little more closely shortly. Now, the Luke holy family were clearly in no hurry to flee from Israel, for according to the religious law of the people of Israel, it was ordained that, after giving birth to a man-child, a mother must go through a period of puri-fication for 40 days: 'She shall touch no hallowing thing, nor come into the sanctuary, until the days of her purifying be fulfilled' (Leviticus 12:4) and, in the case of this holy family, there was no reason not to obey this law. Herod the Great's decree no longer threatened the life of the Jesus of the Nathan line for he had died before the child was born.

*

Before considering further differences between the two nativity accounts, let us look a little more closely at the two Marys.

We do not know who were the parents of the Mary of Luke's Gospel. Regardless of whether Mary grew up in Nazareth itself or in the verdant Galilean surroundings, we can picture her as a young girl growing up in an area which Emil Bock describes as being 'an earthly replica of the Garden of Paradise ... Much more important than the genealogy from which she had physically descended was the celestial background of her soul.'[16] We are reminded here of the words in The Revelation of John which speak of the Queen of Heaven: 'And there appeared a great wonder in heaven; a woman clothed with the sun, and the moon under her feet, and upon her head a crown of twelve stars' (12:1).

From Luke's Gospel we can sense that Mary was a pure and innocent young soul, imbued not with intellectual knowledge nurtured from early childhood by temple priests, but with a wisdom springing from a selfless, love-filled heart. In two places, following the Adoration of the Shepherds and after the twelve-year-old Jesus had been found in the temple, Luke's Gospel says: 'But Mary kept all these things, and pondered them in her heart' (2:19, 51).

Of all the artists it was above all Raphael who revealed the youthful purity, overflowing devotion and love, and the heavenly quality of the Mary of Luke's Gospel. For example, the *Sistine Madonna* and the *Madonna di Foligno* embody the very divinity of Mary herself and the angelic, heavenly origin of the Jesus child. Several of Raphael's paintings of this Mary and her child show them surrounded by the tranquillity and beauty of nature—the world of innocence in which Mary herself had grown up (e.g. the *Small Cowper Madonna*). Raphael also draws our attention to the close relationship between the Jesus child and John the Baptist, the son of Mary's cousin, Elizabeth, for several of his most beautiful works show Mary and the two boys together, surrounded by the soothing, restful green and blue colours of the world of plants and the heavens above (e.g. the *Alba Madonna*).

Whereas the Mary of Luke's Gospel was a 'young soul' who lived what we could call a 'hidden life', the 'other Mary', of Matthew's Gospel, led a more 'open life', not in an insignificant community such as Nazareth but in the city of Jerusalem.

Various apocryphal Infancy Gospels (*The Book of James, or Protevangelium; The Liber de Infantia, or Gospel of Pseudo-Matthew*; and *The Arabic Gospel of the Infancy*), also legends such as those to be found in Voragine's *The Golden Legend* describe the character and life of the parents, Joachim and Hannah (Anna), and the early life of their daughter, Mary, born to them in their old age. (These are wonderfully portrayed by Giotto at the height of his powers in the Scrovegni Chapel in Padua.)

We learn that Mary was taken to the temple by her parents

when she was only three years old. From *The Gospel of Pseudo-Matthew* we hear that at that very young age she walked with the step of an adult, was in complete command of the language and eagerly learned the hymns of praise of the Lord. One would not have taken her to be a little child but a grown-up, say, 30 years old, for she was so earnest and fervent in prayer.

We are told that she 'climbed up the 15 steps without turning around once, and without seeking her parents as children [of the age of three] are otherwise wont to do'.[17]

The legends of her childhood give the strong impression that she not only met the stringent demands of the priests who taught her, but also, as already intimated, displayed a remarkable degree of piety and devotion in her life of prayer. She showed such maturity and independence during the ensuing ten years or so in the temple that it is clear she was already 'in possession of what is normally only the result of many levels of education and inner advancement. Early on, the Mary of the Gospel of Matthew manifested as an 'old soul [...] she represents the polar opposite to the young Mary of the Gospel of Luke'.[18]

*

Let us now consider some other considerable differences between the two nativity accounts. Here, incidentally, we need to remember that the other two canonical Gospels do not mention the birth of the Jesus child. Both Mark and John begin their Gospels with quite a different 'birth'—the baptism of Jesus by John the Baptist in the River Jordan—the incarnation of Christ. An alternative rendering of Luke 3:22 (quoted below) runs: 'There came a voice from heaven, "My Son art thou; this day I have begotten thee." '[19]

In Luke's Gospel the shepherds hear the word of the angels

proclaiming that the child will be born in the city of David, Bethlehem, and that they would find the babe wrapped in swaddling clothes, lying in a *manger*, because there was no room for them in the inn. It is worth noting here that Luke does not mention that the ox and the ass, which bore Mary to Bethlehem, were present in the cattle stall. They were later additions made in the eighth or ninth century (see the apocryphal *Gospel of Pseudo-Matthew*) and were intended to show that the child was the expected Messiah, for in Isaiah it is written: 'The ox knows its owner, and the ass his master's crib' (1:3). However, although the ox and the ass are not mentioned in Luke's Gospel, the presence of the ass by the manger as so often portrayed by artists is certainly in accord with Luke's account, for it was on the back of an ass that Mary would have journeyed from Nazareth to Bethelehem. Rudolf Frieling[20] reminds us, moreover, that the ass was always the symbol of the human physical nature, whose task it is to carry the human being's higher natures on earth. St Francis of Assisi called his body 'Brother ass'. The prophet Zechariah foretells that the Messiah will come riding on an ass (Zechariah 9:9), meaning that he would descend into the realm of corporality. According to the Gospel of Matthew, Christ entered the holy city of Jerusalem riding on an ass (Matthew 21:5). It was also Isaiah who prophesied that 'a virgin shall conceive and bear a son, and shall call his name Immanuel' (Isaiah 7:14).

Quite a different picture is given to us in Matthew's Gospel. There we hear that the three Magi, the Three Wise Men from the East, are led by the star to a *house* in Bethlehem where they find the holy family.[21] There is no mention of a manger. The Matthew Joseph and Mary were domiciled in Bethlehem. The house the three Magi entered was that of Joseph of the Solomon line.

In Luke's Gospel it is Mary who is spoken of as being the recipient of messages from the heavenly world. The archangel Gabriel appears to her, in Nazareth, announcing that she would give birth to a son, to the Saviour. The archangel also told Mary that, in her old age, her cousin, Elisabeth, who was 'of the daughters of Aaron'[22] (Luke 1:5), who had remained childless, was six months pregnant with a son. We then also hear that Mary, now newly pregnant herself, undertook the long journey to a town in the uplands of Judah in order to visit her kinswoman, Elisabeth. We then learn that the baby leapt for joy in Elisabeth's womb at the sound of Mary's greeting. What we see here is John the Baptist's instantaneous recognition of the significance of the child in Mary's womb. This momentous event—not mentioned by Matthew—foreshadows what was to take place 30 years later in the River Jordan, when John baptizes and recognizes Christ. He it is of whom John the Baptist has already declared: 'I indeed have baptized you with water, but he shall baptize you with the Holy Ghost' (Luke 3:16). In Matthew's Gospel we hear that when Jesus comes to John to be baptized, the Baptist exclaims that he rather needs to be baptized by Jesus Christ (3:13–14). In John's Gospel we hear that although the Baptist did not at first recognize who Jesus was, he was nevertheless the first to witness 'the Spirit descending from heaven like a dove, and [that] it abode upon him' (1:32). Twice, in the same Gospel, we hear the Baptist exclaiming, 'Behold the Lamb of God,' (1:29, 36) when he sees Jesus Christ by the River Jordan.

It is revealing to compare the role which the father figure plays in the two Gospels. In the Gospel of Luke Joseph plays a minor role, as it were. In the first two chapters dealing with the Jesus child's infancy Joseph's name is mentioned only in passing. In addition to the Annunciation when Joseph is not present, we also learn that Mary stayed with Elisabeth for about three months and then returned 'to her own home'. We are not told that Joseph accompanied her during all this time. When Mary and Joseph bring the child to the temple in Jerusalem it is to Mary alone that Simeon speaks: 'This child is destined to be a sign which men reject; and you too shall be pierced to the heart. Many in Israel will stand or fall because of him, and thus the secret thoughts of many will be laid bare' (Luke 2:34–5).[23] There is no mention of Simeon's prophetic words in Matthew's Gospel.

Whereas our attention is hardly drawn to the Nathan Joseph in Luke's Gospel, we find that the Solomon Joseph plays a far more active role, is more central stage, in that of Matthew.

Immediately after Matthew has given us an account of Joseph's ancestry we learn that Mary was with child before their marriage had taken place and that he, Joseph, being a man of principle and at the same time desirous of saving his young wife-to-be from public exposure, was minded to have the marriage contract set aside quietly. But that night an angel appeared to him in a dream and said: 'Joseph do not be afraid to take Mary home with you as your wife. It is by the Holy Spirit that she has conceived this child' (Matthew 1:20).

After the three Kings had departed, Joseph has another dream in which he is told by an angel to take the child and his mother immediately to the ancient land of wisdom, Egypt, for Herod the Great commanded that the child should be found and killed.

It is entirely in harmony with the essence of the Solomon Jesus child that he, Mary and Joseph should take refuge in Egypt. For it was in Egypt that the distant ancestor of the Solomon child, King Solomon, renowned for his wisdom, had married an Egyptian princess. In addition, Joseph, one of the twelve sons of Jacob and the first-born son of Rachel

(Genesis 30:22–4), after having been sold by his older brothers to a caravan of Ishmaelite traders, was taken to Egypt where he became adviser to the Pharaoh, married the daughter of the Potiphera priest[24] of On (Genesis 41:45) and eventually had his father with his entire family move from Canaan to Egypt. Jacob's family of 70 (Genesis 46:27) multiplied into many thousands before Moses led his people, the Hebrews, out of slavery in Egypt towards the Promised Land.

Moses, too, had a close bond with Egypt. The first decades of his life were coloured by the mysteries of Ancient Egypt. In the New Testament Stephen says of him: 'Moses was learned in all the wisdom of the Egyptians' (Acts 7:22). In the fragments of the Egyptian historian, Menetho (third century BC), a priest of Heliopolis, we hear that Moses was an initiated disciple of the Mysteries of Heliopolis, the City of the Sun, where Joseph, the son of Jacob, had once received his initiation, for he, Moses, had 'become the son' of the Pharaoh's daughter, and grown to adulthood in the court of the Pharaoh (Exodus 2:6–11).

The first mention of Heliopolis—called On in the Old Testament—is in Genesis where we read that the Pharaoh made Joseph the son of Jacob ruler over all the land of Egypt. On is to be remembered not only as the home of Joseph but, according to a Coptic tradition, as the place to which his far-off namesake took Mary and the infant Jesus early in the sojourn in Egypt. It is true that when they arrived there, having crossed the Sinai desert, the temple complex no longer existed. However, it does not seem unreasonable to assume that some people could still have been encountered there who continued to cultivate the ancient priestly sun-wisdom. Due to background and education, both the Joseph of the Solomon line and the Mary of Matthew's Gospel—tended and

taught in the temple in Jerusalem—would have been in possession of knowledge of the Mystery wisdom that had prevailed in such a cult centre as Heliopolis.

There are several utterances in the Old Testament which
prophesy the Flight from Bethlehem where there was no safe
place for the Solomon Jesus child to lay his head, and the
eventual return of the refugees from their sanctuary in Egypt.
For instance, 'Out of Egypt have I called my Son' (Hosea
11:1). Isaiah predicted the effect the holy child was to have on
Egypt: 'Behold, the Lord rides on a swift cloud, and will come
into Egypt, and the idols of Egypt will totter at his presence'
(19:1).[25]

Emil Bock comments that a whole tapestry of imaginative
tales has been woven around the flight of the holy family into
Egypt.[26] A large part of the conception formed of this flight
has arisen by carrying the mood of the Gospel of Luke into
that of Matthew. Thus painters of, say, the late Middle Ages
and later created many 'Lukelike' pictures of the flight into
Egypt, as if it were the family of Luke's Gospel who was
travelling through the desert of Sinai. Giotto's beautiful
picture in the Lower Church of the Basilica of St Francis in
Assisi may serve as an example of such a portrayal.

After Herod the Great's death an angel appeared again to
Joseph in a dream and told him that he should take his wife
and the child back to Israel. Hearing that Herod's son
Archelaus 'did reign in Judaea in the room of his father'
(Matthew 2:22), Joseph feared for the life of the Jesus child.
We then hear that Joseph has a further dream, as a result of
which he does not return with the mother and child to his
house in Bethlehem, but settles in the small town of Nazareth
in the region of Galilee.

So, in Matthew's Gospel, Joseph assumes a far more active
part than that portrayed in Luke's Gospel. Interestingly this

distinction between the Solomon Joseph and the Nathan Joseph is very often made manifest in the realm of art. In the scene of the Adoration of the three Kings, Joseph is shown either standing, fully alert, gazing down upon the child in Mary's arms or receiving the gifts for the child from the three Kings—gold, frankincense and myrrh. (Plate 1: Fra Angelico, *Adoration of the Magi*, National Gallery, London.) In the scene with the three shepherds Joseph is very often shown sitting on the ground and seemingly unaware of the shepherds' presence. (Plate 2: Matteo di Giovanni, *Nativity*, Pinacoteca, Siena.) What we see represented in so many works of art (including icons of the Eastern Orthodox tradition) is a confirmation that Joseph was not the 'real' father of the Nathan Jesus child. Luke emphasizes this a second time in the third chapter of his Gospel where he opens the genealogy of the Nathan line with the words 'and Jesus himself began to be about thirty years of age, being (*as was supposed*)[27] the son of Joseph' (Luke 3:23, my italics). Commenting on an early sixteenth-century icon of the Cretan School, John Baggley, an Anglican parish priest, makes the following observation: 'At the bottom left corner sits Joseph, the one who is not the father of the child, and who represents those who cannot comprehend the wonder of this event which is beyond the natural order of things. In some icons the devil disguised as an old shepherd stands in front of Joseph tempting him to disbelief.'[28]

It is also significant that the artist's portrayal of the two Jesus children is, more often than not, entirely different. We have already noted that in Matthew's Gospel there is no mention of a manger in a stable. Typically, in pictorial portrayals, the Nathan Jesus child is shown lying on his back, either on his mother's lap, in the manger, or—on occasion— on the straw-strewn earth itself. Often a light, a spiritual light, is shown radiating from this child, dispersing the darkness around him. The *Arabic Gospel of the Infancy* tells us of this light: 'And behold, the cave[29] was filled with shining light whose sparkling radiance was more beautiful than the radiance of all lamps and candles and that shone more brightly than the light of the sun'. (Plate 3: Lorenzo Monaco, *Nativity*, Metropolitan Museum of Art, New York.)[30] In the National Gallery, London, there is a remarkable small panel painting attributed to the Dutchman Geertgen tot Sint Jans ('Little Gerard of the Brethren of St John').[31] The Jesus child lies naked in a coffin-like, rough-hewn manger. From him rays of light fan upwards into the darkness. The radiance is so potent that Mary and the angels ranged round the manger gaze in spellbound awe at the child. The candle held by Joseph appears to give no light at all. Lorenzo Monaco, Geertgen, and other artists, particularly of the fifteenth century, probably based this aspect of their portrayal of the birth of the Nathan Jesus child on the visionary writings of St Bridget of Sweden (1302/3–73) which were published shortly after her death and became known throughout Europe. She witnessed the painless birth of the child and declared that the baby 'radiated such an ineffable light and splendour that the sun was not comparable to it, nor did the candle that St Joseph had put there give any light at all, the divine light totally annihilating the earthly light of the candle'.[32] This same bright light is also shown in Rembrandt's pictures of the Adoration of the Shepherds one of which is in the National Gallery, London.

In John's Gospel we hear that John the Baptist bore witness to the Light. Right at the beginning of his Gospel John the Evangelist writes of Christ as being the Light that shines in the darkness, 'and the darkness comprehended it not'. On several occasions in that Gospel we hear Jesus Christ saying of himself: 'I am the Light of the world.'

The Solomon Jesus child is portrayed quite differently. Characteristically, he is sitting or standing upright, on his mother's thigh(s), with his right hand stretched out towards one or other of the Kings, his fingers in the gesture of blessing. (Plate 4: Sandro Botticelli, *Adoration of the Magi*, National Gallery of Art, Washington, DC).

Often the two quite different accounts of the birth of the Jesus child have been joined together. An example of this can be seen in Sandro Botticelli's painting of the *Adoration of the Magi*, where an ox is plainly visible, standing in the building to the right of Mary (as seen by the viewer). (A clear example of the two accounts being joined together can be seen in Botticelli's *The Mystic Nativity* in the National Gallery, London.) As has been mentioned already, the presence of this animal is not mentioned in the Gospel of Matthew, nor is it consistent with the status of the Solomon Joseph—as a man of some wealth he would have had a separate shelter for his animals.

In this portrayal of the Adoration, as in many others by Italian artists, we are confronted by a house—often of grand proportions as befits a man of some substance—in ruins. On this theme James Hall comments:

The idea of the New Dispensation (Christianity) growing out of, or superseding, the Old (Judaism) was sometimes represented in later medieval art by the image of a building, the Synagogue, being dismantled and its bricks and stones used to construct a church, the New Jerusalem. The motif of the ruined building, with this symbolic meaning, came to be particularly associated with the scenes of the Nativity of Christ and Adoration of the Magi [. . .] In Italian Renaissance painting its style tends to be classical, and may here be regarded as symbolizing the decay of paganism.[33]

*

It was mentioned earlier that the visit by the three Magi with their retinues to the house of Joseph was a very public occasion, whereas the visit to the stable by the humble shepherds was an intimate happening that went unnoticed by the public at large. There is a remarkable painting by Fra Angelico and another by Fra Filippo Lippi[34] which illustrate clearly how the trappings of the royal birth described by Matthew obscure the humble birth described by Luke.[35] What Botticelli, the two monks, and numerous other artists, have done is to combine the two distinct stories of the Gospels of Matthew and Luke into an event which in reality took place at different times and at different locations in Bethlehem.

The Nathan child, born in the obscurity of a simple family and worshipped by the simplest of men, is himself an expression of utter simplicity and 'newbornness'. The Solomon child, a prince of the royal house of David, attended by kings, bears in himself a spirit of great maturity and regal wisdom. In Blakean terms we could say that in the Matthew-Solomon child we see Experience, in the Luke-Nathan child Innocence. William Blake opened his introduction to *Songs of Innocence* with the lines:

Piping down the valleys wild,
Piping songs of pleasant glee,
On a cloud I saw a child,
And he laughing said to me:

'Pipe a song about a lamb!'
So I piped with merry chear (*sic*).
'Piper, pipe that song again';
So I piped: he wept to hear.

Here we may sense the flavour and mood of the simple shepherds watching their sheep by night and the newborn child lying in the manger.

In Blake's introduction to his *Songs of Experience* we find a contrasting mood:

Hear the voice of the Bard!
Who Present, Past, & Future sees;
Whose ears have heard
The Holy Word
That walk'd among the ancient trees,

Calling the lapsed Soul,
And weeping in the evening dew;
That might controll (*sic*)
The starry pole,
And fallen, fallen light renew!

In these lines we may sense the spirit of wisdom of the three Magi from the East and the spiritual maturity of the royal child of the Matthew Gospel.[36]

*

From what we have seen so far, the Nathan or Luke child is closely associated with the temple and therefore with the priesthood. Not only does the first chapter of Luke's Gospel open with an account of the father-to-be of John the Baptist, Zacharias, who was a priest and to whom the archangel Gabriel appeared in the temple and announced that his aged wife, Elisabeth, who 'was of the daughters of Aaron',[37] would give birth to a son, but, in the second chapter, we hear that the newborn Jesus child is taken by Mary and Joseph to the temple in Jerusalem to be presented to the Lord and that Simeon 'came by the Spirit into the temple'. It had been revealed to him by the Holy Ghost that he would not die 'before he had seen the Lord's Christ'. He recognizes the Jesus child as the Saviour and, praising God, prays that he might now depart life in peace. He then speaks earnestly to Mary in terms we have considered already. This second chapter in Luke's Gospel closes with the scene of the twelve-year-old Nathan child in earnest discussion in the temple with the temple teachers. 'And all that heard him were astonished at his understanding and answers' (Luke 2:47).

Towards the end of his Gospel, Luke repeatedly draws our attention to Christ's teaching in the temple: 'And he went into the temple, and began to cast out them that sold therein, and them that bought; saying unto them, It is written, My house is the house of prayer: but ye have made it a den of thieves. And he taught daily in the temple' (Luke 19:45–7). In the final two verses of chapter 21 Luke writes: 'And in the day time he was teaching in the temple; and at night he went out, and abode in the mount of Olives. And all the people came early in the morning to him in the temple, for to hear him.' Luke again mentions Christ's teaching in the temple in the following chapter. After giving an account of Christ's betrayal by Judas we hear that Christ said to the high priests and elders: 'Be ye come out, as against a thief, with swords and staves? When I was daily with you in the temple, ye stretched forth no hands against me' (Luke 22:52–3). Christ's preaching in the temple is, of course, mentioned in Matthew's Gospel, but far greater emphasis is laid upon this activity in that of Luke.

Rudolf Frieling writes of Luke as being the evangelist of prayer. He refers to the priest Zacharias making the incense offering in the interior of the temple, while the devout community outside accompanies his deed with their prayer:

It is as if this incense-scented prayer was permeating the entire Gospel of Luke's which, at its conclusion, leads us back into the temple. 'And they worshipped him and returned to Jerusalem in great joy, and they were continually in the temple praising and glorifying God' (Luke 24:53).

In relation to the Jordan Baptism, Luke—and only Luke—mentions the praying of Jesus, which here, too, is of crucial significance (Luke 3:21). Frieling adds that soon after Jesus had begun his public activity, it says: 'He withdrew into the wilderness and prayed' (Luke 5:16; also Mark 1:35). And yet another peculiarity of Luke: the ascent up the mountain, prior to the choosing of the twelve apostles, is for him the elevation to a great nocturnal prayer. 'He went up into the mountain to pray, and all night he continued in prayer to God' (Luke 6:12).[38]

It is worth noting here that in the Western tradition the mountain, the mountain-symbol, appears in the 'legend' of the Grail as Montsalvat—the 'Mountain of Salvation'. In general, the mountain, the hill and the mountain-top are all associated with the idea of meditation, spiritual elevation and the communion of the blessed. It was on Mount Horeb that Moses heard the voice of the Lord. All four Gospels speak of Christ going 'up into a mountain' to pray.

William Wordsworth describes his experience of the power of the spirit when he reached and rested for a while on the top of Mount Snowdon:

A meditation rose in me that night
Upon the lonely Mountain when the scene
Had pass'd away, and it appear'd to me
The perfect image of a mighty Mind.

The Prelude, 13:66–9

E.R. Smith[39] makes the following interesting statement regarding the meaning of 'mountain' in esoteric writings:

It is important that we understand the meaning of *mountain* in spiritual writings. It is universally recognized by the enlightened as meaning the condition in which one has an experience beyond or above that of the world of the senses . . . It is not necessary to be on a physical mountain in order to be *on the mountain* in a spiritual sense.

*

There is no mention of the temple in Matthew's account of the infancy of the Jesus child. The Magi from the East come to Bethlehem seeking him who is 'born King of the Jews'. Almost immediately after his birth, the jealous, power-ridden, megalomaniac king Herod the Great seeks to have the royal child assassinated, so the family flee to Egypt.

Now, one of the most obvious symbols of kingship is the *throne*.[40] Whereas it is characteristic that the Nathan child is depicted in Christian art either in a manger or lying on straw or a garment on the earth, the Solomon child, as has been mentioned already, is frequently shown sitting or standing on his mother's knees, with his right hand raised in the gesture of blessing. This is a typical portrayal in Byzantine art (Plate 5: Icon, *Mary with Jesus Child Enthroned*, Heraklion, Crete, 1450–1500, Monastery of St John the Theologian, Patmos). In Italy we see the Byzantine influence finding expression in the majestic paintings of such artists as Cimabue, Duccio and Giotto, where Mary is portrayed as sitting on a throne (Plate 6: Cimabue, *Mary with Jesus Enthroned*, Galleria di Palazzo Pitti, Florence). A very early representation, in mosaic, of the enthroned Madonna and Child is to be seen in the basilica Sant'Apollinare Nuovo[41] in Ravenna. Here we see the three Magi, richly garbed and wearing the characteristic trousers and Phrygian caps of the Persian priests, advancing towards the enthroned Madonna and Child, bearing the gifts of gold, frankincense and myrrh (Plate 7). A much earlier representation (wall painting) of the three Magi, garbed as in Ravenna, was found in the second half of the twentieth century in a catacomb under the Via Latina in Rome.[42]

It is in accord with the whole tenor of Matthew's Gospel that he lays far greater stress on the emblem of the throne than Luke in his. For instance, Matthew tells us that, addressing his disciples, Christ spoke of the time to come 'when the Son of man shall sit in the throne of his glory' (Matthew 19:28).[43]

*

Here it is of interest to note that with the triumph of Christianity in the fourth century and the proclamation at the Council of Ephesus (431)[44] of Mary as *Theotokos,* the Mother of God, the way was opened up for picturing the Mother and Child as inspired by imperial iconography. There multiplied in the East as well as in the West—inspired by the Byzantine world—images called *Maestà,* i.e. of the Mother seated upon a throne presenting the Jesus child to the world.

This iconographic model gave rise in the Byzantine world to two kinds of representation of Mary and the child, both equally regal. One is the *Panagia Nikopeia,* where Mary is standing or seated, severe and majestic. She is holding the Jesus child who, facing the world, is raising his right hand in the gesture of blessing and, in his left hand, holds the sacred scroll[45] (see Plate 5). The other is the *Panagia Hodigitria* ('She who points towards the Way') where the Mother is depicted either seated or standing, or with the upper body alone shown, her right hand pointing towards the Child.[46] (Plate 8: *Mary and Jesus Child,* 1400–40, Church of Nicholas Orphanos, Thessaloniki). The Jesus child, most often given the features of a child more mature than those of a newborn child, is seated upright on his mother's left arm. His right hand—this has already been mentioned in connection with the child of the Solomon line—is raised in the gesture of blessing, and in his left arm he is frequently shown holding the scroll of the Bible. One tradition speaks of the newborn Solomon child being able to read. Of the Nathan child we hear, at the beginning of the apocryphal *Arabic Infancy Gospel*, that he could speak as soon as he was born. To his mother, Mary, he said: 'I am Jesus, the Son of God; I am the Logos.' Referring to this passage Bock writes:

> Leaving aside the fact for the moment that we hear of the miracle of early speech, nevertheless from the beginning an atmosphere must have prevailed around the child as if the Logos, the Creative Word from which all things are made, was present above and in him, as if, through this child, one could look back into the pure, divine beginnings of all evolution, into the beginnings of Creation.[47]

*

It is pertinent to note here that, historically, all Christian Churches celebrated the birth of Jesus on 6 January until the fourth century. According to Roman Catholic sources, the date was changed from January 6 to December 25 in order to overshadow a pagan feast dedicated to the birth of the Sun which was celebrated on 25 December. So, the Church hierarchy designated December 25 as the official date of Christmas and 6 January as the feast of Epiphany, the Baptism in the Jordan—the incarnation of the Christ. The Armenian Church, however, was not a satellite of the Roman Church, and Armenians have continued to celebrate Christmas, the Nativity, on 6 January until today. Nor has the Coptic Church adopted the date of 25 December but has always celebrated the Nativity during the night of 6/7 January. In the

Holy Land the Greek and Russian Orthodox Churches also celebrate Christmas on 6 January.

*

The last we hear of the boy Jesus in the Gospels is in that of Luke. There we are given an account of the event that took place in the temple at Jerusalem in the twelfth year of the life of the Nathan Jesus.

We learn that Mary and Joseph, together with many others from Nazareth, were accustomed to visiting the temple every year at the feast of the Passover (Luke 2:41–51). When the Nathan Jesus reached the age of twelve—the official coming of age[48]—he, and the Solomon Jesus child, went with them. When the parents of the Nathan Jesus started out on the journey home, he—and the older boy—stayed behind. He was not missed until the party had made a whole day's journey back to Nazareth. Mary and Joseph returned to Jerusalem. After three days[49] they found him in the temple, discoursing with the teachers, who were amazed at his understanding and the answers he gave to their questions. Mary and Joseph, too, were amazed at his intelligence and the answers he gave to the learned men gathered around and listening to him.

From Luke's unique account we may assume that the Nathan Jesus had been in the temple for three days. It is clear that during that period a significant change had taken place in the twelve-year-old. Luke does not reveal what actually had happened. Ovason[50] makes the following pertinent point:

> The account is unique to Luke, and one has the impression that if the passage were to be removed, little would be lost from the story of the childhood of Jesus. In fact, nothing could be further from the truth. The event in the temple is

of primary importance, not so much for what is said by Luke, but for what he implies. The surprising thing is that Luke takes only 52 verses to describe the Nativity and childhood of his Jesus, yet he dedicates 21 of these to the events in the Temple.

In regard to the fact that Luke does not tell us what actually happened in the temple, Ovason goes on to say:

In this respect Luke was merely observing the established tradition in such matters. It had always been forbidden to write or speak openly about the pagan Mysteries, and Luke seems to have felt the same silence to be incumbent upon him in the face of the new Mysteries.

As we have noted already, Mary and Joseph were astonished to see and hear the boy in the temple. Mystified would perhaps describe their reaction better, for what had taken place in the temple may be described as a Mystery. That there must have been a change in the Nathan Jesus boy seems apparent. Why would Mary and Joseph have been so amazed to find him discoursing with men of learning if this had not been so? We need to remember here that the Nathan Jesus had grown up in a humble household in Nazareth. Joseph was a carpenter, not a man of great learning. But at the age of twelve Jesus had arrived at the threshold of manhood and recognized what his mission on earth should be, for—according to Luke—when Mary asks him, 'My son, why have you treated us like this? Your father and I have been searching for you in great anxiety,' he told her that he had to be about his Father's business, that he was bound to be in his Father's house, in his temple. The relationship with the Heavenly Father of which the twelve-year-old Nathan Jesus is conscious is portrayed in numerous works of art. For instance, in the painting by

Matteo di Giovanni[51] *The Virgin and Child* we see God the Father looking down upon them from the heavenly heights. In this work of art we also see the moment of the Annunciation; the archangel Gabriel is on God the Father's right and the Virgin on his left as seen by the viewer (Plate 9: Museo di Collegiata di Sant'Agata, Asciano; the painting was originally in Sant'Agostina). Seen in the light of the twelve-year-old Nathan Jesus boy's statement regarding his 'Father's house', the enigmatic phrase we meet in the third chapter of Luke's Gospel where it is said that Jesus 'was supposed' to be the son of Joseph makes perfect sense. A small picture in the Museo di San Marco, Florence, by Fra Angelico, shows not God the Father but Christ—the Cosmic Christ[52]—with a cruciferous halo, looking down upon Mary who is standing with the Jesus child in her arms (Plate 10). Another small picture by the same artist, also in the Museum of San Marco, depicts the Cosmic Christ looking down from the heavens upon Mary at the moment of the Annunciation.[53] Are we not reminded here of Christ's words 'I and my Father are one' (John 10:30), and also of the opening sentences of John's Gospel? A fascinating page in the illuminated Gospel of Bishop Bernward of Hildesheim (*c.* AD 1000) shows the Cosmic Christ—with cruciferous halo—present at the birth of the Jesus child. He is holding a scroll in his left hand with the single word 'Vita' written on it. 'In him was life; and the life was the light of men' (John 1:14). His right hand supports a lamb—also with a cruciferous halo—one of the most frequently used symbols of Christ in all periods of Christian art. (Plate 11.) Many scriptural passages give authority for this symbolism. A typical reference is John 1:29: 'The next day John [the Baptist] seeth Jesus coming unto him, and saith, Behold the Lamb of God, which taketh away the sin of the world.'

In one of the apocryphal Infancy Gospels, the *Gospel of*

Thomas,[54] the event in the temple is also mentioned. The terms in which it is portrayed are more emphatic than those we find in Luke's Gospel. The modest portrayal by Luke of Jesus in discussion with the men of learning is replaced by such expressions as: 'And after the third day they found him in the temple sitting in the midst of the doctors and hearing and asking them *questions*. And all men paid heed to him and marvelled how that being a young child he put to silence the elders and teachers of the people, expounding the heads of the law and the parables of the prophets.'

After mentioning how Jesus responded to his mother's grief and reproach, Thomas goes on to report: 'But the scribes and Pharisees said: Art thou the mother of this child? And she said: I am. And they said unto her: Blessed art thou among women, because God hath blessed the fruit of thy womb. For such glory and such excellence and wisdom we have neither seen nor heard at any time.'[55]

*

Let us now consider a few of the statements made by Rudolf Steiner in his spiritual research into the nature and qualities of soul of the two Jesus children. The idea of two Jesus children was discussed by him on a number of occasions, starting in 1909, a year before the so-called *Damascus Document* was first published[56] and many years before the discovery of the Hebrew and Aramaic scrolls at Qumran (from 1947 onwards), and before the Coptic scrolls were discovered in 1945 in upper Egypt. The Qumran scrolls, in particular, have supported Rudolf Steiner's view. We shall consider one or two aspects of the latter in due course.

In a lecture he gave in Basle in September 1909[57] Steiner developed for the first time his account of the significant differences between the two Jesus children described by Luke and Matthew. One of the profoundest differences was based on an esoteric view of history which can only be mentioned in passing here—a more detailed statement is beyond the scope of this introductory study.[58] In short (and certainly inadequately expressed) Steiner's esoteric view is that the two children represented separately the impulses behind Buddhism (Luke)—the Gospel of St Luke is a profound expression of love and compassion—and the wisdom stream of Zoroastrianism (Matthew), and that they 'combined', became one, in the twelve-year-old Jesus of Nazareth discoursing with the teachers in the temple. This Nathan/Solomon Jesus eventually became the vehicle for the Christ during the three years of his ministry on earth.[59]

Here it is apposite to quote a passage from the late Canon[60] A.P. Shepherd's book *A Scientist of the Invisible*:

> Steiner . . . reveals that it was not until his thirtieth year that Jesus was fully developed as Son of Man and that the eternal Christ-being entered into his physical body and united himself with it. This happened at the baptism in the Jordan. This was a widely held view in the early Church, and is expressed in the Epistle to the Hebrews in the quotation from the fortieth Psalm, 'A body didst thou prepare for me! Lo, I am come to do thy will.' However, through a materialistic conception of reality, this view led to heresies in which the true union of the divine and human natures in Christ Jesus was denied. In consequence, the point in earthly time at which the Christ actually entered into the physical nature of Jesus was put back to his birth and even to his conception.

According to Steiner in several of his lectures on the Gospel of Matthew (1910), the Matthew Jesus child was an incarnation of the Zarathustra-individuality who lived and taught in ancient Persia.[61] There are several documents we can refer to here which support his contention. For instance, in the apocryphal *Arabic Gospel of the Infancy* it is pointed out that it was the fulfilment of a Zarathustra prophecy proclaimed by the stars, following which the Three Wise Men, the Magi, embarked on their journey: 'And it came to pass, when the Lord Jesus was born at Bethlehem of Judaea, in the time of King Herod, behold, Magi came from the East to Jerusalem, as Zorodasht [i.e. Zarathustra] had predicted.' Now, there is some evidence that Steiner was familiar with the New Testament apocryphal *Arabic Gospel of the Infancy*,[62] but nowhere in his written works and over 6000 lectures did he mention the remarkable works by thirteenth-century Syrian theologians, among whom were Mar Solomon and Bar Hebraeus. Both of these scholars lend support to Steiner's view of the connection of the birth of the Matthew Jesus child with the wisdom stream of Zarathustra.[63]

Mar Solomon, metropolitan of the Syrian-Nestorian Church in the thirteenth century, gives us a description in his book known as *The Bee* not only of the Messianic prophecy by Zarathustra, but he also clearly states that the Jesus child of Matthew's Gospel is the reincarnated Zarathustra:

The prophecy of Zorodasht [Zarathustra] concerning our Lord . . . : He said to his disciples, King Gushnasaph, Sasan and Mahimad: 'Hear, my beloved children, for I will reveal to you a mystery concerning the great King who is about to rise in the world at the end of time. A child will be conceived in the womb of a virgin, and shall be formed in her members, without any man approaching her . . . for he is a child conceived by the Word which establishes natures [i.e. the Creator of all beings].

Gushnapash asks him: Is he greater than thou, or art

thou greater than he? Zorodasht says to him, *He shall descend from my family; I am he, and he is I; he is in me, and I am in him ... He and I are one* [my emphasis].

Zorodasht's answer to Gushnapash's question is in accord with Steiner's statement mentioned earlier that the Zarathustra-individuality incarnated in the Hebrew people as the Solomon Jesus.

In his book *The Beginnings of Christianity* Andrew Welburn observes that discoveries at Qumran and Nag Hammadi (1945) have led many scholars to a conclusion reached by Steiner in 1910:

> At many junctures in these writings, lurking just on or beneath the surface, we meet the expectation that Zarathustra, the great spiritual master of Iran and founder of the Zoroastrian religion, will be reincarnated as a great 'Illuminator' in several nations in succession, and finally in Palestine.

Welburn then goes on to say that the most arresting of the Nag Hammadi texts from our present viewpoint is the *Apocalypse of Adam*.[64] Adam prophetically reveals that Zarathustra—the Illuminator—will go through a number of incarnations. The thirteenth rebirth of Zarathustra would be as the Saoshyant in Palestine, there to become the vessel of 'the Undefiled One of truth' or 'the great Saviour'.

In the *History of the Dynasties* by Bar Hebraeus, a Syrian scientist and Jacobite bishop (1226–86), there is a passage where the Zarathustra of the sixth century BC is described as a Messianic prophet:

> In this age, there lived Zorodasht, the teacher of the sect of magicians [i.e. Magi] ... He taught the Persians about the coming of Christ and directed them to offer up gifts to him.

He proclaimed to them: In the last days, a virgin will conceive a child and when it is born, a star will appear that shines during the day, and in its midst will be visible the form of a virgin ... So when you behold that star, make ready to go where it will lead you and, adoring it, offer up your gifts to the child. The child is the 'Word' which has established the heavens.

The writers of Ancient Greece rendered the name Zarathustra in a Greek version, namely, Zoroaster, which means 'Gold Star'. It is this Star[65] the three Magi followed to the house of Joseph in Bethlehem. It should be noted that Matthew was the only one to speak of the *Star* (Matthew 2:1–12). It is an interesting fact of history that when in AD 614 the Persians invaded Palestine, although the land was devastated and Jerusalem reduced to rubble, they spared the birthplace of the Jesus child (the fourth-century Church of the Nativity is on the assumed site) and the early home of King David, because the Wise Men from the East, on their pilgrimage following the Star, were portrayed wearing Persian garb.

Zarathustra's prophecy to which Bar Hebraeus refers is expressed in the text of the Avesta (nineteenth yasht):

The mighty one, bearing the royal promise,
The sun-ether-aura, created by God,
We worship in prayer,
That will be transferred to the most victorious of redeemers
And the others, his apostles,
Who further the world,
That enables them to overcome age and death,
Decay and putrefaction,
That helps them to eternal life,
To thrive eternally,
To free will,

When the dead rise again,
When the living conqueror of death comes,
And through his will the world will be advanced further.[66]

Here is clearly expressed that the divine Spirit of the Sun 'will be transferred' to a unique human being who will be the Redeemer for all mankind, will heal and overcome death.

*

We need now to pause before continuing with the theme of the two Jesus children, and look a little more closely at the significance of the pre-Christian civilizations' esoteric perception of the divine Spirit of the Sun, of God revealed through the essence of light.

The Sun, the Spirit of the Sun, has been adored by human beings for thousands of years. The type and the details of this worship have varied in different ages and in different parts of the world. It was not the physical sun which was the object of the adoration of the various pre-Christian civilizations; it was, as Jacob Streit expresses it, 'the eye and the raiment of the divine, was a revelation of the highest principle of the earth and mankind and the cosmos'.[67] Someone (if one may use the word) must first be there who is capable of expending this celestial largess—someone 'behind' the sun. John, in his Gospel, calls this 'someone' the Word, in Whom was Life, Light and Love.

The ancient Indians spoke of Surya Deva ('the shining one'), who moved across the heavens in a chariot drawn by a team of four or seven horses.

The ancient Persians knew the Spirit of the Sun as Ahura Mazda (Ormuzd). It was the primal Zarathustra (who lived thousands of years before his reincarnation,[68] in the sixth century BC, as the initiate spoken of by Mar Solomon and Bar

Hebraeus as Zorodasht), who, looking up at the sun, saw the Christ Spirit, whom he called Ahura Mazda, behind the physical sun, behind the sunlight. Ahura Mazda was worshipped as the Spirit of Light, who was opposed to the Spirit of Darkness. Light and rhythms of time taught the ancient Persians to till the soil and conquer its darkness. Geoffrey Ashe suggests that 'the ethics taught by Zarathustra were based on the social life of the husbandman. The good man [was] one who looked after the cattle and tilled the soil in peace and neighbourliness'.[69] Whereas the ancient Indian had experienced the material world as an illusion, the ancient Persians, under the guidance of Zarathustra, were taught to regard it and understand it as a reality, as a reality permeated by spirit. The spiritual world itself was light, the material world offered resistance to this light, and the quality of resistance was darkness.

As mentioned already, the noble, priestly leader of the ancient Persians, the primal Zarathustra—as distinct from the later Zarathustra (Zorodasht) spoken of by Mar Solomon and Bar Hebraeus—may have lived several thousand years before Christ. The Zend-Avesta itself, in the form in which it has come down to us, is estimated to be not older than around 700–600 BC. The original thoughts of the primal Zarathustra were handed down for many generations by word of mouth before they were written down. There seems little doubt that in the course of time new material would have accrued. However, the kernel of the primal Zarathustra's teaching regarding Ahura Mazda, the divine Light and 'Word' of the Sun as source of All, remained central throughout.

The ancient Egyptians worshiped the Sun Being in different forms, under different names. Among the most important sun gods were Re (or Ra), Atum, Horus and, during the reign of Amenhotep IV (Akhenaten), Aten (or

Aton). Aten was represented as the sun's disc with rays terminating in hands. Re was the self-engendered Eternal Spirit.
Having created himself, he turned his attention to the
creation of the world and humankind. The 'means' used by
Re—whose chief centre was at Heliopolis, the City of the
Sun—in the creation of the world, and all that is in it, was the
Word. Here we are reminded of the first words in the Gospel
of John: 'In the beginning was the Word, and the Word was
with God, and the Word was God. The same was in the
beginning with God. All things were by him [i.e. the Word,
Christ]; and without him was not any thing made that was
made. In him was life; and the life was the light of men' (John
1:1–4).[70]

The Egyptians also believed that certain animals possessed
divine powers, which led to the cult of sacred animals, birds
and reptiles, each of which was considered to be the mani-
festation on earth of a divine being. So we find, for example,
that Horus, an Egyptian god, was depicted either as a falcon
or with the head of a falcon on a human body. Another
Egyptian god, Chnum, was portrayed as a man with a ram's
head; Thoth, the god of wisdom, had the head of an ibis, and
so forth. It was this aspect of Egyptian religion that the
Greeks found curious and the Romans horrifying. Being
polytheistic themselves, both Greeks and Romans accepted
Egypt's polytheism. Their own gods, however, although
celestial, immortal beings, were nevertheless recognizably
human. They had beautiful human bodies and were possessed
of human emotions and frailties.[71]

For a very short period in the history of ancient Egypt
polytheism was set aside. Amenhotep IV, better known as
Akhenaten, established monotheism. He replaced the myriad
deities of his land with one god—Aten (Aton). Akhenaten
was in advance of his time—a forerunner of the advent of

Christ. The solar cult of the god Re (Ra), developed in Heliopolis, paved the way for Akhenaten's crusade to establish the sun as sole god. But, however evident the Heliopolitan origin of the new state religion might be, it was not merely sun-worship of the god Re, for the word Aten implied more than the great vital force of the sun itself, a visible reality. Akhenaten believed the invisible essence of the Divine Being 'dwelt' in the visible body of the sun disc. Aten was the giver of life, and the source of all life on the earth. His symbols were the heat and light of the sun which vivified and nourished all creation.

Akhenaten's *Hymn to the Sun* is claimed to be the first truly monotheistic composition in the literature of the world. The following few lines from this majestic hymn give some idea of Akhenaten's conception of Aten:

O Living Aten who creates life
. . .
O sole God, who is like none other,
You made the earth according to your will, alone.
Men and women, cattle and beasts,
Everything on earth that walks upon feet,
Everything above that flies with its wings
. . .
You alone, rising in your form as the living Aten,
Appearing and shining, far off, yet close at hand
From out of yourself alone you have made myriad
    forms...

Part of a limestone relief (now in the Cairo Museum) from the great temple at Amarna shows Akhenaten and his wife, Nefertiti, worshipping the Aten (Aton). Rays, descending from the disc of Aten, terminate in hands, some of which hold the symbol of life, the *ankh*. The back of Tutankhamun's gilt

throne shows the young Pharaoh with his wife, Ankhesena-
mun. Again we see rays from the sun, the source of all life,
terminating in hands, two of which are holding a *crux ansata*
(the *ankh*) under the nostrils of the young couple.

Out of Egypt came the children of Israel. Although Moses,
their leader, had been brought up in the court of the Pharaoh
and been immersed in the wisdom of Egypt and the cult of the
worship of the Spirit of the Sun, he came to perceive the
power of the Spirit of the Sun through the mediation of
thunder and lightening, in fire, air and the clouds. Inspiration
came to him on the mountain and before the burning bush.
Out of the element of fire the Lord, Christ, said to Moses 'I
AM THE I AM', *ehjeh asher ehjeh* (Exodus 3:14). When the
Yahweh (Jehovah) deity revealed himself to Moses in the
burning bush and on Mount Sinai, the same divine power was
encountered that had earlier proclaimed itself to the Egyptians in the figure of Osiris. The divine entity, known to the
ancient Egyptians as Osiris, had come closer to the earth.

Osiris, the representative of the Spiritual Sun, was betrayed
and killed by his brother Seth (Set). Through the love and
loyalty of his wife, Isis, Osiris was restored to life, was
resurrected. One tradition speaks of Isis, having the ability to
change herself into a kite, creating a powerful flow of air by
flapping her wings and thereby breathing new life into Osiris.
From then onwards Osiris ruled in the realm of the afterlife.

The death and resurrection of Osiris in a spiritual body
prefigured the event of the death and resurrection of Jesus
Christ. Osiris, however, was not Christ himself. But we may
say that the Christ Being appeared through and in him.

In ancient Greece the Spirit of the Sun was known as
Phoebus Apollo/Helios. In Greek times the Sun, the Spirit of
the Sun, came closer to men and women on earth. The heaven
of the Greek gods, Mount Olympus, was the whole living

Sun-filled ether, a spiritual realm that 'touched' and 'surrounded' the earth. Gods and humankind drew nearer to one another.

Phoebus Apollo (Phoebus means 'the bright one', 'the shining one') was synonymous with the sun in later classical writers, although for Homer Apollo was distinct from the sun god Helios. The Sun Spirit Apollo brought healing and love to mankind. The love of wisdom became philosophy, *philo sophia*.

Apollo was the son of the king of the gods, Zeus, and of Leto. She was forced to leave Mount Olympus and eventually gave birth to Apollo and his twin sister Artemis on the island of Delos in the Aegean Sea. So, according to their mythology, the ancient Greeks envisaged the birth of a god on earth. They also envisaged their gods assisting them in their activities. For instance, Apollo is shown guiding the Lapiths to victory over the Centaurs in the west pediment of the Temple of Zeus at Olympia. He stands, the only static figure, in the centre of the turmoil, invisible to the physical eyes of the combatants on both sides. Another example: in the Trojan War he stands, invisible, at the side of Hector and aids him in his fight against Achilles.

So, Phoebus Apollo, the Spirit of the Sun, moved *invisibly* among men and women on earth.

The worship of Mithras was a last remembrance of the Christ who had not yet reached the earth but was descending. The worship of Mithras was an echo of the old clairvoyant perception.[72]

Over the aeons this Cosmic Being, the Spirit of the Sun, grew closer and closer to the earth and mankind until he finally descended into the physical body of the Solomon/ Nathan Jesus at the Baptism by John. The prophets, who looked towards the time when the Messiah would appear among them, knew that only a very special physical vessel would be able to receive this spiritual Being. They found it had its source in the generations of the Hebrew people, and so they prepared for his appearance. This was the stem of Jesse (the father of King David), 'and a Branch shall grow out of his roots: And the spirit of the Lord shall rest upon him.' This was the prophetic vision of the descent of the Spirit of the Sun, Christ, into a physical body—a descent that took place step by step over a long period of time. The strict Israelite laws concerning the preservation of the purity of the race had been their fully conscious aim. Isaiah said: 'And there shall come forth a body.'

Christ then lived, prayed and taught in a physical body for three years among the people of Palestine.

Before the Baptism, the Spirit of the Sun, the Spirit of Christ, had been on a long descent through the millennia towards the earth and those who dwelt on the earth. The foregoing few paragraphs give some idea as to how this gradual descent may be envisaged.

It has been mentioned already that in the early years of the twentieth century Rudolf Steiner spoke on many occasions of Christ as the Spirit of the Sun,[73] and that over a long period of time this Spirit gradually descended out of the cosmic heights to incarnate in a physical body. For instance, he indicated this in a lecture in 1911. He quoted the following few words of St Augustine:[74] 'That which we now call the Christian religion already existed among the ancients and was never absent from the beginning of the human race up to the time when Christ appeared in the flesh; from that time forward the true religion, which was already there, received the name of the Christian religion.' Steiner went on to say: 'Thus does a standard authority point to the fact that it was not something new which came into humanity with the events of Palestine, but that in a certain sense a transformation had taken place in that which from time immemorial the souls of men had striven for as knowledge.'[75]

Archimandrite Kallistos Ware of the Orthodox Church expresses this reality—from quite a different viewpoint—in the following poignant few words in his Introduction to *The Festal Menaion*: '[We need to see] the Incarnation not as an abrupt and irrational intervention of the divine, but as the culmination of a long process extending over thousands of years.'[76]

In 1923, speaking of the Sun Spirit, the Christ, Steiner made the point that whereas in earlier times human beings were able to look out into the heavens and find the Christ as the Sun Spirit in outer space, since the time of Christ's time on earth we 'must find the way into our own inmost being and along this path find the inner Sun, the Christ.[77] This, surely, is the meaning of Christ's words, as recorded by Matthew in the very last line of his Gospel, 'I am with you always, even unto the end of the world' (28:20).

It is fascinating to realize that the Sun-image has continued to 'represent' the Being of Christ through to our time. Many examples could be found to substantiate this claim. Here just three will be mentioned: the Irish high crosses, St Peter's in Rome and a Romanesque church in Tübingen.

In the centre of the cross in almost all early and late Irish high stone crosses is the Christ. In the oldest the Christ is usually represented by a symbol of the sun. In short, the Christ is identified with the 'light of the world', with the sun.[78] There are many good examples of such crosses, but mention will be made here of two eighth-century crosses at Ahenny (Tipperary) whose west and east faces have a central boss—not, in short, the figure of Christ—and a large circle, which goes through the shaft and the arms of the cross. Still today a circle with a central point is the astronomical symbol used for the sun. At Kilaghtee (Donegal) the cross, at the top of a massive shaft, is contained *in* the sun disc; at Aghowle (Wicklow) the sun disc nearly 'eclipses' the top of the shaft and both the arms of the cross.

On Irish stone crosses we do not meet with the crucified figure as a physical body hanging on the cross in agony, but we see him as the Risen One or, sometimes, as the Giver, the Self-sacrificer. One of the best examples of a twelfth-century cross portraying the Christ is to be found at Kilfenora (County Clare). The Christ figure spreads out his arms in benediction. The sacrificial blood runs down the shaft of the cross in two streams and spreads over the ground, the earth.[79]

*

In the last century, on the ceiling of a chamber from the Pre-Constantine necropolis under the Basilica of St Peter's an early fourth-century mosaic was discovered; it represented Christ in his glorious role as the Sun in his chariot, the Christ-Helios or Sun Christ—the Phoebus Apollo of ancient Greece (Phoebus = shining, bright). On three sides of the chariot and the Christ-Helios are branches of a vine in leaf. The vine as the emblem of Christ follows from his words expressing the new relation between God and humankind through him: 'I am the true vine, and my Father is the husbandman . . . I am the vine, ye are the branches' (John 15:1, 5).

In St Peter's itself there is a remarkable sculpture. It is part of a group by Gianlorenzo Bernini (1598–1680) decorating the tomb of Pope Alexander VII. At the four corners surrounding the enthroned Pope are the four virtues, Charity, Prudence, Justice and Truth. 'Truth' stands with her left foot on a globe of the earth, symbolizing her power over the earth.

What is remarkable is that she clutches in her arms the *sun*—indeed, a *sunburst!*

On the high altar in St Peter's (and in other Roman Catholic churches) stands a magnificent monstrance, also called the 'ostensorium'. It is of gold—others are of silver—finely wrought, with rays radiating from a central circular glass panel through which the Host can be seen. The Roman Catholic Church acknowledges that the monstrance is a sunburst. 'During the Baroque period, it took on a rayed form of a sun-monstrance with a circular window surrounded by a silver or gold frame with rays.'[80]

Blattmann (1985)[81] draws our attention to the medieval walls of St Jacob's Church in Tübingen in which there is a carved stone on which 'there is a strangely impressive picture: *the sun with two hands*'. He also makes the following statement:

> Whoever goes fully along with this and follows our line of thinking will come freshly to the knowledge that was self-evident in early Christian times, and only later fell into oblivion: that what was born and went forth from the Baptism, namely Christ, is the *Sol novus*, the newborn Sun-spirit itself. Common invocations of Christ were *O sol salutis* (sun of salvation), *Helios anatoles* (sun of the rising) and the prophet Malachi, calling Him the 'sun of righteousness' says that He will arise 'with healing in its wings' (Malachi 4:2).
>
> We know now that it is the sun-god, Christ, who dwelt in the man Jesus of Nazareth [...] and that it is truly to him that all the characteristics must be attributed which in earlier times belonged to Sol or Helios or Aton [Aten].

Bearing in mind what has just been said in regard to the Spirit of the Sun and also remembering the three paintings mentioned earlier that depict the brilliant light emanating from the Nathan Jesus child in the manger, a short quotation from a Christmas sermon on the Eucharist given by John Chrysostom (*c.* 347–407) may serve to further illustrate the relevance of Steiner's statements regarding the descent of the Spirit of the Sun:

> This Table [the altar] takes the place of the manger; for here too the Body of the Lord will rest, not, as of yore, clad in swaddling clothes but bright with the radiance of the Holy Spirit. Those who are initiated know whereof I speak [...] Picture to yourselves what it means to behold the Sun that has come down from Heaven to dwell on Earth, letting His radiance shine out from this place over *all* men. But if the Light that is *visible* cannot shine without arousing wonder in the hearts of all who behold it, only consider what it signifies to see the radiance of the *Sun of Righteousness* streaming forth from our own flesh and sending Light into the soul.

*

The Gospels themselves give us ample indications as to the cosmic background of Christ. Already in the accounts of the birth of the Jesus child in the Gospels of Matthew and Luke we find such indications. In Matthew, as we have seen, it is the Star, guiding the Magi, which appears over the birthplace of the holy child. In the Gospel of Luke it is the host of angels who tell the simple shepherds of a heavenly element which is to bring peace on earth to human beings who are of good will.

A further event which emphasizes the cosmic background of the appearance on earth of the Christ Being is the Baptism of Jesus (Matthew 3, Mark 1, Luke 3). The cosmic spheres, the heavens, opened, and the Spirit descended upon the 30-

year-old Jesus. And a voice from on high proclaimed: 'This is my beloved Son, in whom I am well pleased' (Matthew 3).

The cosmic background is revealed again at the transfiguration on the mountain (Matthew 17, Mark 9, Luke 3). Christ's most intimate disciples, Peter, James and John, experience how his appearance changed. According to Matthew, 'He was transfigured before them, and his face did shine as the sun, and his garment was light as the light.' And, as at the Baptism, 'a voice out of the cloud, from the Heavens, from the spiritual world, proclaimed: 'This is my beloved Son, in whom I am well pleased; hear ye him.'

In his book *The Cosmic Christ* Hans-Werner Schroeder points to the fact that at Christ's death on the cross 'images of the cosmic background also arise, this time not in the human appearance but in sun and earth:

'And the earth did quake, and the rocks rent, and the graves were opened' (Matthew 27:52).

According to Mark (15:33) we learn that 'when the sixth hour [noon] was come, there was darkness over the whole land until the ninth hour'.

Luke also speaks of the darkness over the whole earth and then goes on to say: 'And the *sun* was darkened'—that is, lost its light (23:44f).

From the various examples mentioned in these few pages—examples that could be multiplied many times—we may say that Star and, in particular, Sun are salient images for the Cosmic Christ.

*

Let us now return to our main theme—two Jesus children.

The Matthew Jesus child was born of a young mother. We can find a confirmation of this assertion in a passage in two of the apocryphal Infancy Gospels, namely, *The Gospel of*

Pseudo-Matthew and *The Book of James or Protevangelium.*
According to the latter:

> Mary was in the Temple of the Lord as a dove that is
> nurtured; and she received food from the hand of an angel.
> And when she was twelve years old there was a council of
> the priests, saying: Behold Mary is become twelve years old
> in the Temple of the Lord. What then shall we do with her?
> lest she pollute the sanctuary of the Lord. And they said
> unto the high priest [Zacharias]: Thou standest over the
> altar of the Lord. Enter in and pray concerning her: And
> whatsoever the Lord shall reveal to thee, that let us do ...
> And lo, an angel of the Lord appeared unto him: Zach-
> arias, Zacharias, go forth and assemble them that are
> widowers of the people, and let them bring every man a
> rod, and to whomsoever the Lord shall show a sign, his
> wife shall she be.

In the apocryphal *Gospel of Pseudo-Matthew* it is stated
that Mary was 14 years old. Jacobus de Voragine also claims
that Mary was 14 rather than 12 years old.[82] Giotto di
Bondone (1266–1336)—inspired by the apocryphal *Gospel of
Pseudo-Matthew* and that of *The Book of James, or
Protevangelium* and, particularly by Voragine's account in
The Golden Legend—painted a magnificent series of frescoes
(1303–5) in the Scrovegni Chapel, Padua, portraying the life
of the Matthew Mary from her birth to her marriage.

The Nathan Jesus child was also born of a young mother.
We don't know the exact ages of the two Marys when they
gave birth, but, in general, Italian Renaissance artists depict
the Matthew Mary as being somewhat older than the Nathan
Mary. Fra Angelico's painting of the latter, listening to the
archangel Gabriel, shows a very young woman (Plate 12: *The
Annunciation*, Museo di San Marco, Florence). Here we may

remind ourselves that it is only in Luke's Gospel that we hear that 'the angel Gabriel was sent from God unto a city of Galilee, *Nazareth*' (my italics). In Matthew's Gospel we learn that, in a dream, Joseph, domiciled in Bethlehem, 'hears' that his betrothed shall give birth to a very special child.

According to Steiner the Nathan Jesus child, who had not gone through previous incarnations, grew up in such a way that the ordinary human qualities connected with knowledge and understanding of the external, physical world developed very slowly in him. His intellectual capacities were out-weighed by quite other qualities: 'He unfolded a depth of inwardness comparable with nothing of the kind in the world, a power of feeling that had an extraordinary effect upon everyone around him.'[83] 'His soul contained a profundity of innocence and love.'[84] In New Testament apocryphal Infancy Gospels we can read about some of the Nathan Jesus child's activities which bear witness to this. Luke, in his Gospel, speaks of this child as being 'filled with wisdom and the grace of God was upon him.'[85]

One could, perhaps, say that it was the kind of wisdom with which a person is endowed, who lives and works in har-monious communion with nature, a person who does not intellectually probe and analyse, but 'knows' with the forces of his heart. Thus in the Nathan Jesus we see a child with infinite depths of feeling, wisdom of the heart.

In contrast to the Nathan child we could say that the Solomon Jesus child possessed the wisdom of the Magi, of the Three Wise Men from the East. 'He was an individuality of exceptional maturity, having profound understanding of the world,'[86] wisdom of the head. Again, in apocryphal Infancy Gospels we can find this confirmed.

Contrasting the different kinds of experience the shepherds and the Magi had, Steiner made the observation:

In a kind of dream-condition, the simple shepherds in the fields were able inwardly to realize what was drawing near in the event of the birth of Christ Jesus. On the other hand, the knowledge possessed by the three Magi from the East enabled them, by contemplating the phenomena of the heavens, to discern that an event of a significance far transcending that of the ordinary course of life was taking place on the earth.[87]

Characteristic of the Nathan Jesus child is the account given in *The Arabic Gospel of the Infancy* of a young woman being healed of her leprosy by water being poured over her with which his body had been washed; in the same Gospel we hear that, out of clay, he made figures of birds and they flew when he commanded them to fly. Many other pictures of such healing and creative deeds—deeds issuing from a heavenly power of love—are given to us in apocryphal Childhood Gospels.

The profundity of the Solomon Jesus child's knowledge is clearly portrayed in *The Gospel of Pseudo-Matthew*. A learned teacher had asked Joseph to bring the boy to him for tuition. He soon found that he was the pupil and the boy the teacher. So he went to the boy's father and said:

> Brother, I beg of you, take him away from me, for I cannot look him in the face and cannot listen to the earnestness of his words [...] Oh, my friends, I am humbled in my thinking; a victim I am to illusion and to deprivation. I prided myself on having a pupil; but now he is my teacher and my disgrace. I have lost my importance because I have been outdone by a child.

*

Now, we remember that after their return from Egypt, the family of the Solomon line did not return to Bethlehem but settled in the small village of Nazareth—a small 'community' would be a more appropriate term. In both Gospels we hear Nazareth being described as a city (Matthew 2:23; Luke 1:26; 2:39). During the time of Jesus Christ, however, Nazareth was a small village. It is estimated that first-century Nazareth was a community in which perhaps no more than about 30 to 35 extended families dwelt.[88] From very recent excavations, Stephen Pfann, a Bible scholar and archaeologist, concluded that there could have been no more than 35 homes spread over six acres to ten acres. The village of Nazareth would have been a little over 650 yards at its greatest east-west length and about 200 yards at its greatest north-south width.[89] So, whereas today Nazareth is one of the largest cities in Israel, it was tiny in the time of Jesus Christ. (Does this go some way to explain Nathanael's question: 'Can any good thing come out of Nazareth?)[90] The two Jesus children therefore lived in close proximity to one another. The Solomon Jesus child was about twelve months older than the Nathan child.

The theologian and priest Emil Bock, in his seminal work *The Childhood of Jesus,* gives us a picture of how the friendship could have evolved between the two growing boys. He begins by referring to an early Christian tradition, recorded in the works of the Christian Gnostic Justin Martyr,[91] according to which the Jesus child often spent time with the flock as a shepherd boy. Bock then goes on to say:

One can readily picture the Nathan Jesus tending the sheep and goats in the meadows surrounding Nazareth and, while doing so, dreamily looking into the world and sky above. More and more often, the Solomon youngster may have felt drawn to go out and be with him. He felt strangely at ease in the presence of the younger boy. The harmonizing, calming effect which had always emanated from the Luke-child to his environment benefited the Matthew-youngster in a special way. All the restless questions and striving for knowledge in his soul came to fulfilled rest. He himself now learned a little of playing and dreaming; increasingly, a profound change made itself felt in his nature ... Out of the love for this friend, his heart forces now developed and grew, the forces that gradually balanced his powerful faculties of reason and consciousness.

In the other boy, too, a change took place through contact with the friend. While by nature he possessed great receptivity and permeability for the images and sounds that passed before his senses, now the beginnings of an interest for thought elements and things of the mind were aroused in him as he listened to the words of the older youth. It was as if he were learning not only to see with his own but with the sense organs of the other. And so he acquired a share in the wakefulness of mind with which all perceptions of his friend were imbued. Even as the Solomon youngster felt increasingly drawn to seek the closeness of the other boy's being, so a growing longing arose in the Nathan-youth to share in the far more conscious soul contents of the other ... The Solomon boy felt blessed that he could linger in the heavenly soul atmosphere; that with all his thoughts he could live in the soul of the friend. The other felt marvellously filled and enriched in that he was able to receive and harbour in his own being the older friend's utterly different ego with all its wealth of consciousness.[92]

*

Though Matthew's Gospel does not tell us that the Solomon family went to the Feast of Passover in Jerusalem, it would seem more than likely that they were in the large party that undertook the journey from Nazareth and its environs at the same time as the Nathan family. It is not improbable that the two Jesus boys—the Solomon Jesus boy being about a year older than the Nathan Jesus boy (some scholars consider that the difference in age between the two boys could have been greater than this[93]—were in the temple at the same time. Steiner's interpretation indicates that they were, as do also many portrayals by artists in the fifteenth and sixteenth centuries.

Steiner describes how, in the temple in Jerusalem, the Nathan Jesus child, all soul and heart, received into himself the spirit and thinking power of the Solomon Jesus child. As a consequence of this Mystery event, the Solomon child was depleted of his life-forces and died shortly after it had taken place. The Nathan Jesus, on the other hand, was now so wise that the learned men in the temple 'were amazed at his intelligence and the answers he gave' to their questions (Luke 2:47).[94] The keenest capacities of wisdom of the head, of the brain, such as only a descendant of the house of Solomon could develop, were united with the purest love forces of the heart of the Nathan Child. The kingly and the priestly powers were united in the Nathan Jesus child and formed the chalice into which, 18 years later, at the Baptism by John in the River Jordan, the Christ Being descended or, as Luke describes this moment, 'the heaven was opened, and the Holy Ghost descended in a bodily shape like a dove upon him, and a voice came from heaven, which said, Thou art my beloved Son; in thee I am well pleased' (Luke 3:22).[95]

The twelve-year-old Nathan Jesus became aware of his future mission on earth during the three days in the temple. We remember that in answer to his mother's troubled questioning when he was found in the temple he answered her, according to Luke, with two questions: 'How is it that ye sought me? wist ye not that I must be about my Father's business?' His true Father, the twelve-year-old is saying, is not Joseph but God. He was already aware of the reality of the divine message which would issue from the heavenly heights at his baptism. (See pp. 62–3 and 64–6.)

It is significant that Luke observes that Mary and Joseph did not find the missing twelve-year-old for *three* days. In the ancient Mysteries, for instance, in Egypt, Ephesus and Eleusis, some of the more important and secret ceremonies performed during the process of initiation lasted for three days. In both Egyptian and Greek Mysteries such ceremonies involved an experience equivalent to a kind of 'death' during which the soul and spirit of the candidates undergoing the final stages of the process left the physical body, and a new inner life, enriched by spiritual knowledge, spiritual wisdom, was bestowed upon them. The ceremonies and processes involved in these Mystery centres could not be divulged to anyone not considered spiritually mature enough. In fact, they were a closely guarded secret. In this connection Frederick Hiebel, in his book *The Gospel of Hellas,* reminds us that the Greek dramatist Aeschylus (*c.* 525–*c.* 456 BC) was accused by the Areopagus of betraying the Eleusinia in *Prometheus Bound.* This middle part of Aeschylus' great trilogy—and the only part of it preserved for us—grew out of the dramatist's contact with the Mysteries of fire and with Hephaestus, the god of fire and metals.

It is clearly not a matter of an ordinary initiation ceremony which took place in the temple during the three days in Jerusalem. But perhaps we may see here the culmination of a process that had been growing between the two Jesus boys in their life together in Nazareth. The star-wisdom, the cosmic wisdom, of the kingly Solomon Jesus child was bestowed upon the Nathan Jesus child. Or, as Steiner states, it was

1. Fra Angelico, Adoration of the Magi (National Gallery, London)

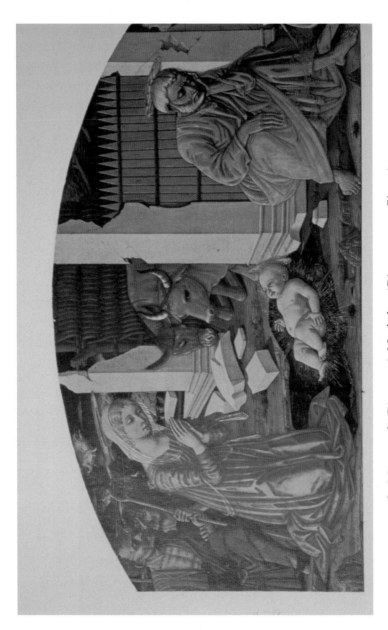

2. Matteo di Giovanni, Nativity (Pinacoteca, Siena)

3. *Lorenzo Monaco, Nativity (Metropolitan Museum of Art, New York)*

4. *Sandro Botticelli,* Adoration of the Magi *(National Gallery of Art, Washington, DC)*

5. Icon: Mary with Jesus Enthroned *(1450–1500, Heraklion, Crete, Monastery of St John the Theologian, Patmos)*

6. *Cimabue,* Mary with Jesus Enthroned
(Galleria di Palazzo Pitti, Florence)

7. *Mosaic*: Adoration of the Magi (*Sant' Apollinare Nuovo, Ravenna*)

8. Mary and Jesus child, Panagia Hodigitria
(1400–40, Church of Nicholas Orphanas, Thessaloniki)

9. *Matteo di Giovanni,* The Virgin and Child
(Museo di Collegiata di Sant' Agata, Asciano)

*10. Fra Angelico, Mary, standing, and Jesus child
(Museo di San Marco, Florence)*

*11. The Cosmic Christ witnessing the birth of the Jesus child
(from the illuminated Gospel of Bishop Bernward of Hildesheim,
c. AD 1000)*

12. *Fra Angelico, The Annunciation (Museo di San Marco, Florence)*

13. Raphael, Madonna del Duca di Terranuova
(Dahlem Gallery, Berlin)

*14. Ambrogio Bergognone, Twelve-year-old Jesus in the temple
(Museo di Sant' Ambrogio, Milan)*

15. Defendente Ferrari, Twelve-year-old Jesus in the temple. Detail. (State Gallery Stuttgart)

during the three days in the temple that the mature, higher spirit of the Solomon Jesus left his body and passed into the body of the Nathan Jesus. Another way of expressing this could be: the stellar wisdom possessed by the three Magi from the East was given over to the harmoniously developed nature-love, earth-love, with which the simple shepherds were imbued. The wisdom of the Magi, imbued with reverence and understanding, united itself with the love, imbued with piety and humility, of the shepherds.

*

Several of the apocryphal New Testament books hint at the Mystery of the two Jesus children. For instance in the *Gospel of the Egyptians* it is said that when Salome asked when the Kingdom (salvation) will come, the Lord answered: 'When the Two become One.' This statement also occurs in *The Second Epistle of Clement* where it is followed by the words 'and the Exterior like the Interior'. Salvation depends on the Two becoming One. The Two become One when, in the temple, the individuality of the Solomon Jesus passed over into the Nathan, and qualities that had been entirely inward became outward.[96]

*

The Gnostic text *Pistis Sophia* (third century AD) contains a fascinating account of an incident from Jesus' childhood which is highly relevant to the theme of the 'Two becoming One'. It is put into the mouth of Mary. She narrates it in order to explain the fulfilment of the saying, which she quotes: 'Surely his salvation is at hand for those who fear him, that glory may dwell in our land. *Mercy* and *truth* are met together, *righteousness* and *peace* have kissed each other [my italics]. Truth shall spring out of the earth;

and righteousness shall look down from heaven' (Psalm 85:10–11):

> When you were small, before the Spirit had come upon you, while you were with Joseph in one of the vineyards, the Spirit came from on high and came to me in my house, looking like you, and I did not recognize him, and I thought it was you. And the Spirit said to me, 'Where is Jesus, my brother, that I may meet him?' When he said this to me, I was perplexed and thought it was a ghost come to tempt me. And I seized him and bound him to the foot of the bed which is in my house, until I went out to you both, to you and Joseph in the field and found you in the vineyard, while Joseph was fencing in the vineyard.
>
> Now it happened that you heard what I said to Joseph, and when you understood you were glad, and said: 'Where is he, that I may see him? For I await him in this place.' And it happened that, when Joseph heard you say these words, he was perplexed, and we went up together, entered the house, and found the Spirit bound to the bed. And we looked at you, and at him, and found that you resembled him. And when he who was bound to the bed was freed, he embraced you and kissed you, and you kissed him, and you both became one.

If we approach this apparently fantastic 'imagination' and hold in our minds the content and inner meaning of the Psalm Mary quoted, we can perceive its relevance in regard to the theme of the two Jesus children. Bock gives us an insightful commentary:

> In the supersensibly exact manner in which the two concepts 'mercy and truth' and 'righteousness and peace' are used in the *Pistis Sophia,* they precisely recount the spiri-

tual nature of the two Jesus souls. The Solomon Jesus is the bearer of 'truth', the wisdom acquired in the evolutionary history of mankind; the Jesus of the Nathan line is pure 'mercy', heavenly being that gives of itself. The Solomon Jesus bears within himself 'peace', the highest quality that humanity can grow towards on their own; the Nathan Jesus bears within himself 'righteousness', the radiant sun glory of higher existence which cannot, of itself, bestow itself on earthly man, for he lost it in paradise, but which the 'new Adam' brings with him to earth as the Christ-being's soul garment. They encounter each other, they kiss and become one; in them, earthly man ('will spring up from the ground') and heavenly man ('righteousness will look down from the sky') become one.[97]

Andrew Welburn comments: 'In these somewhat anecdotal reflections on the part of the mother of Jesus, it may yet be that we possess a refraction of esoteric and Gnostic traditions concerning what happened to Jesus at the age of twelve.'[98]

*

Since the discovery of the Dead Sea Scrolls at the Essene settlement at Khirbet Qumran, near the shores of the Dead Sea, beginning in 1947 (nearly 40 years after Rudolf Steiner had first spoken of two Jesus Children), it has become more generally known that the Essenes[99] awaited not only a Prophet and a Messiah[100] but three Messianic figures: King, Prophet and Priest. Matthew's nativity story corresponds to the Essene expectation of a royal Messiah and Luke's birth of Jesus to the priestly Messiah—with John the Baptist assuming the role of the Prophet. In a similar way in which the Christians saw Jesus Christ fulfilling the messianic roles of both the Davidic king and high priest, so also the Essenes saw the need for a messianic figure to fulfil both roles. They, however, unlike Christians, saw not one 'anointed one' but two 'anointed ones'—one a secular ruler (Davidic king), and the other a high priest.

A passage which speaks of the two Messiahs[101] in the early publishing of the Qumran manuscripts is to be found in the document known as *The Community Rule*. It reads: '[They] shall be ruled by the primitive precepts in which the men of the Community were first instructed until there shall come the Prophet and the Messiahs of Aaron [the high priest, of the tribe of Levi][102] and Israel [the Davidic king].'[103]

A similar strain of dual Messianism is evident in one of the Qumran documents known as *The Damascus Document*. Extensive fragments were recovered from three Qumran caves. Two incomplete medieval copies of this document had been found already in 1896–7 (amongst a mass of discarded manuscripts in a storeroom of an old Cairo synagogue). They were published in 1910, a year after Steiner spoke for the first time of the two Jesus children. In this Qumran document, which may be dated to the second century BC, there are three references to the coming of the two 'anointed ones', the two Messiahs of Israel and 'of Aaron, of the tribe of Levi'.[104]

This understanding of two Messiahs is also apparent in the document known as *The Messianic Rule*[105] where an eschatological communal meal is described:

> The Priest-Messiah shall summon them. He shall come at the head of the whole congregation of Israel with all his brethren, the sons of Aaron the Priest, those called to the assembly, the men of renown; and they shall sit before him ... And then the Messiah of Israel shall come, and the chiefs of the clans of Israel shall sit before him ... And when they shall gather for the common table, to eat and to

drink new wine ... let no man extend his hand over the first-fruits of bread and wine before the Priest; for it is he who shall bless the first-fruits of bread and wine, and shall be the first to extend his hand over the bread. Thereafter, the Messiah of Israel shall extend his hand over the bread.

The 'Messiah of Israel', the Davidic king, is clearly distinguished here from the 'Messiah of Aaron', the high priest. It is also clear that the King has to take second place to the Priest.

In the *Commentary on Isaiah* we find that the royal Messiah, the 'David Messiah', was to rule under the guidance of the priestly Messiah. Another scroll, the *Messianic Florilegium*, refers to the 'David Messiah' (the kingly Messiah) and the 'Teacher of the Torah' (the priestly Messiah).

An Essene work, well known long before the discoveries at Qumran in 1947, which perhaps more than any other emphasizes the Messianic duality, is the *Testaments of the Twelve Patriarchs*. Here the dying words of the twelve sons of Jacob are recorded. According to the *Testaments*, which could date to the third or late second century BC, the Messianic high priest is expected to come from the tribe of Levi, and the political or 'kingly' Messiah to come from the tribe of Judah. Here we should remember that Aaron, the founder of the priesthood, was of the tribe of Levi.[106]

The *Testaments* contain frequent references to the expectation of two Messiahs. Here just three statements will be mentioned.

In his *Testament* Simeon, the second-born son of Jacob and Leah,[107] exclaims: 'And now, my children obey Levi, and in Judah shall ye be redeemed: and be not lifted up against these two tribes, for from them shall arise to you the salvation of God. For the Lord shall raise up from Levi as it were a Priest, and from Judah as it were a King, *God and man.* So shall *he* save all the Gentiles and the race of Israel' (my italics).[108]

Levi, the third-born son of Jacob, addressing his dying words to his sons, glorifies the advent of the priestly Messiah:

> Then will the Lord raise up to the priesthood a new Priest, to whom all the words of the Lord shall be revealed; and he shall execute a judgment of truth upon the earth, in the fullness of days. And his star shall arise in heaven, as a king shedding forth the light of knowledge in the sunshine of day, and he shall be magnified in the world until his ascension. He shall shine forth as sun in the earth. The heavens shall rejoice in his days, and the earth shall be glad, and the clouds shall be joyful, and the knowledge of the Lord shall be poured forth upon the earth, as the water of seas; and the angels of the glory of the presence of the Lord shall be glad in him.

Judah the fourth-born son of Jacob and Leah exhorts his children to love Levi:

> And now, my children, love Levi, that ye may abide, and exalt not yourselves against him, lest ye be utterly destroyed. For to me the Lord gave the kingdom, and to him the priesthood, and he set the kingdom beneath the priesthood. To me he gave the things upon the earth; to him the things in the heaven. As the heaven is higher than the earth, so is the priesthood of God higher than the kingdom upon the earth.[109]

In some of the *Testaments of the Patriarchs* we can discern a teaching of a Priest and King in one. One instance of this is to be found in Levi's *Testament.* In a vision Levi heard seven men in white raiment saying to him:

Arise, put on the robe of the priesthood, and the crown of righteousness, and the breastplate of understanding, and the garment of truth, and the diadem of faith, and the tiara of miracle, and the ephod[110] of prophecy. And each one of them bearing each of these things put them on me, and said, From henceforth become a priest of the Lord, thou and thy seed for ever. And the first anointed me with holy oil, and gave the rod of judgment. The second washed with pure water, and fed me with bread and wine, the most holy things, and clad me with a holy and glorious robe. The third clothed with a linen vestment like an ephod. The fourth put round me a girdle like unto purple.[111] The fifth gave me a branch of rich olive. The sixth placed a crown on my head. The seventh placed on my head a diadem of priesthood, and filled my hands with incense, so that I served as a priest of the Lord.

The *Messianic Anthology* (4Q *Testimonia*), usually dated to the middle of the first century BC, was found near the site of Khirbet Qumran in the early 1950s. The text includes four quotations connected by interpretation. The first two quotations from Deuteronomy (5:28–9, and 18:18–19) refer to the raising up of a prophet like Moses. The third is an extract from a prophecy of Balaam about the royal Messiah (Numbers 24:15–17), and the fourth is a blessing of the Levites and, implicitly, of the Priest-Messiah (Deuteronomy 33:8–11).[112]

It is clear, from documents discovered at Qumran, that the Essenes expected two Messiahs, two anointed ones, to appear.

Welburn points out that in the later Essene texts the hope of a single embodiment of priesthood and kingship seems to have receded. However, this hope is expressed again in an early Christian writer, Hippolytus of Rome, who evidently knew the Essene secret teaching and saw it fulfilled in Jesus Christ. 'He interpreted the different genealogies of Jesus advanced in the Gospels to signify the coming together of two lineages, each with its prophetic justification.'[113] Welburn then quotes two passages from Hippolytus' commentary *On the benedictions of Isaac, Jacob and Moses*:

[It was prophesized] that the Christ would be born, according to his bodily descent, from the tribe of Levi, from the priestly order, from the house of Aaron ...

Welburn comments: 'Yet the usual tradition makes the Messiah a royal figure, descended from Judah! Hippolytus, however, is in the possession of prophecies which he believes can reconcile the two versions:'

For we have found it written that the Christ must also appear from the tribe of Levi, as a priest of the Father, from a commingling of the tribe of Judah with the tribe of Levi, so that the Son of God should be made known from both as King and as Priest.[114]

Welburn continues:

The scriptural derivation of the dual promise from the blessings uttered by Moses in the book of Deuteronomy is exactly that employed in the Essene *Messianic Anthology*. It is therefore a virtually definite assumption that the Essene teaching has been handed down within Christianity, and is being made known by Hippolytus. We know too that the *Testaments of the Patriarchs* were prepared for use by Christians. And after Hippolytus' time, the idea was accepted and taken up by the highly influential Ambrose[115] in his book *On the Patriarchs* (*De patriarchis*). We are therefore in the presence of a line of Essene secret teaching which continued within Christian circles.

A recent clear exposition of the Essene doctrine of the two Messiahs is that presented by the German Roman Catholic theologian Karl Georg Kuhn. He states:

The concept of the two Messiahs, a priestly and a political one, is actually not as strange as it first appears to be. The entire structure of postexilic Israel shows the side-by-side position of the priestly hierarchy and a worldly political leadership. This structure is given already in the juxta-position of the 'princes' as worldly leaders, found in Ezekiel 44–6. In Zechariah 4:14 (c. 520 BC) we see, side-by-side, the Aaronite Joshua, the high priest, and the Davidic Zerub-babel, the worldly leader of the Israelite community, as 'the two anointed ones'.[116]

The passage in the Old Testament book of the prophet Zechariah to which Kuhn refers runs:

I said unto him [the Lord], What are these two olive trees upon the right side of the candlestick and upon the left side thereof? And I answered again, and said unto him, What be these two olive branches which through the two golden pipes empty the golden oil out of themselves? And he answered me and said, Knowest thou not what these be? And I said, No, my lord. Then said he, These are the two anointed ones, that stand by the Lord of the whole earth (Zechariah 4:11–14).

Although there is no actual mention of the two Jesus children, the Zohar, a segment of the Cabbala, contains numerous passages like the following: 'The son of David and the son of Joseph are two, not one.' 'Another Messiah, the son of Joseph, shall unite with the Messiah, the son of David. But the Messiah, the son of Joseph, will not remain alive; he will be slain and will come alive again when the little mound receives light on the great mound.'

Bock, commenting on these and other passages, says that it is as if 'someone were groping in a dark room for something and catches hold of nothing but chaotic contours of what can only be recognized in the light of day'.

*

The New Testament itself makes no mention of the Jesus children knowing each other in Nazareth, nor does it mention that the Solomon Jesus was in the temple with the twelve-year-old Nathan Jesus. The artistic tradition, however, has been less reticent. We shall be considering just two works of art depicting the Nathan Jesus discoursing with the learned men in the temple.[117] First, however, let us look at a well-known painting by Raphael, the *Madonna del Duca di Terranuova* (Plate 13).

There are three small boys in this painting. One of the children is young John the Baptist. He has all his usual attributes: a cross, a garment of camel's hair,[118] a halo and the *Agnus Dei* scroll.[119] It has been mentioned already that the lamb as a symbol of Christ is one of the most frequently used in all periods of Christian art.

On the lap of Mary is the Nathan Jesus child. He and John the Baptist hold between them a scroll with the words which will be used by John when they meet again as adults by the River Jordan: 'Behold the Lamb of God, which taketh away the sin of the world' (John 1:29). To the left of Mary another little boy, standing, is leaning against her. He is clearly somewhat older than the boy of the Nathan line. Like the boy on Mary's lap and John, he also has a halo. He is the Jesus of the Solomon line. It need not really surprise us that the two Jesus boys are found together here, for Joseph of the Nathan line returned with Mary and the child to his home in Nazareth after the presentation at the temple in Jerusalem, and, as we have already learnt from Matthew's Gospel, we know that on their return to Israel from Egypt, Joseph of the Solomon line took Mary and the child to Nazareth.

Bock, referring to this painting by Raphael, comments:

> One need not necessarily conclude that Raphael possessed a clear knowledge, formulated in thoughts, of the two Jesus children, even though we would by no means rule this out completely. It is possible, perhaps in connection with a secret tradition among painters, that the inspired feelings of the artist may have caught hold of an image that was spiritually accurate.[120]

In an endeavour to find an explanation for the presence of the young haloed boy standing to Mary's left, he has been interpreted by many scholars as being James, the brother of the Solomon Jesus, mentioned in Mark's Gospel (6:3). However, the argument against such an interpretation is twofold. In the first place Raphael shows the standing boy as being somewhat older and more mature than the boy resting on his mother's lap and, in the second place, we learn from both Matthew (1:25) and Luke (2:7) that the Jesus child mentioned in their Gospels is the mother's first-born. In the light of the thesis put forward in these pages, it would seem that we are confronted here by the two Jesus children, the Nathan child *and* the Solomon child, who is 'somewhat older'.

In both apocryphal writings referred to above the Joseph mentioned is of the Solomon line. Now we know that the Solomon Jesus child was born at least a year before the

Nathan Jesus child (some authorities suggest he could have been two or three years older). James, the youngest son of the widower Joseph, was older than the Solomon Jesus child and Raphael, who like most Italian Renaissance artists would have been familiar with the apocryphal writings, would therefore have depicted him as being older than the boy he placed to Mary's left if he had meant the boy to represent Joseph's son James.

Here it is relevant to note that in Luke's Gospel there is no mention of siblings; this only occurs in the Gospels of Matthew (13:55) and Mark (6:3).[121] Archimandrite Kallistos Ware, of the Russian Orthodox Church, in his Introduction to an English translation of the Festal Menaion, points out: ' "Brother" is here understood by Orthodox to mean half-brother—perhaps children of Joseph by a previous marriage—or else cousin or other close relative.' When we turn to the New Testament apocryphal writings we find it very clearly stated, in the *Book of James, or Protoevangelium,* that Joseph considered himself to be far too old to be the young Mary's husband. He was a widower: 'And Joseph refused saying: I have sons.' In the *History of Joseph the Carpenter, or Death of Joseph,* we learn that Joseph had four sons, Judas, Josetos, Simon, James, and two daughters, Lysia and Lydia. 'His wife died, leaving James still young.'

In the museum of the Church of Sant'Ambrogio in Milan there is a fresco by Ambrogio Bergognone (1450–1523)[122] (Plate 14) depicting the twelve-year-old Nathan Jesus in the temple. It illustrates the moment when his mother Mary and Joseph discover him in the temple in Jerusalem after searching for him for three days (Luke 2:46–52).

Jesus is shown seated. On either side of him are the learned men. He has his left hand raised—a gesture indicating that he is explaining something. The significant departure from the traditional composition of the temple theme as given to us in Luke's Gospel (2:46–52)—depicted, for instance, by Duccio di Buoninsegna (1260–1319)[123]—is that Bergognone shows Mary leading a *second* Jesus boy away, even while the twelve-year-old Nathan Jesus boy is still speaking from the podium. The premise that we are here confronted by two distinct Jesus boys is based on three significant factors. First, Bergognone is not representing continuity within a story by depicting two or more actions of one and the same person, for the convention of continuous representation requires that actions that are separated chronologically must also be given their individual, separated spaces. Bergognone has not complied with this requirement. Indeed, as Ovason points out, 'the device of continuous representation was outmoded by Bergognone's time'. Second, although the two boys resemble each other in appearance, they are not the same. The boy on the left of the picture, upon whom Mary is gazing down with loving concern, appears depleted of energy. We notice that both are clothed in red shifts. However, the shift of the boy leaving the temple is paler in colour than that of the twelve-year-old seated in the centre. Both are making similar gestures, though those of the departing Jesus boy are much weaker; his left arm is not held up and outwards but, palm downwards, hanging limply towards the ground. This weakened gesture is reflected in his face. In comparison with the Jesus boy in the chair of the teacher, the departing boy appears wan and ailing. We notice, too, that the halo of this boy, the Solomon Jesus, is far less brilliant than that of the teaching Nathan Jesus. And, thirdly, the two Jesus boys are clearly aware of each other. In particular, we can recognize the bond between the two boys by the way in which the Nathan Jesus looks down upon the departing Solomon Jesus with what Ovason calls 'a strange mixture of love and wistfulness'. He goes on to say: 'The

Solomon child seems to have sacrificed something of his spirit, something of his being to the Nathan child, and consequently is suffering.' According to Steiner the Solomon Jesus died very shortly after this event in the temple.[124] It is clear that it is not solely the Nathan boy who is aware of his departing friend, for nearly all, if not all those learned men who a moment before had been discoursing with the twelve-year-old on the podium, now have their attention directed towards the boy who is about to leave the temple with Mary and Joseph.

Bergognone seems to have had some esoteric knowledge of which other Italian artists, particularly in the late fifteenth and first half of the sixteenth century, were also cognizant. We find other representations of the twelve-year-old in the temple by, among others, Gerolamo Giovenone (c. 1490–1555), Martino Spanzotti (before 1456–1526/28) and Defendente Ferrari (fl. 1518–35). A picture by the last named artist, in the State Gallery in Stuttgart, shows the listening Solomon Jesus youth, with his face turned ardently upwards, leaning on the left arm of the twelve-year-old teaching Nathan Jesus who is majestically enthroned in the middle. Mary, Joseph, and the two Jesus boys are distinguished by a halo. However, the halo of the discoursing Nathan Jesus is not the usual round disc but a radiant sunburst. The two Jesus boys are similar in appearance, but whereas the enthroned Nathan Jesus looks strong and confident, there is a suggestion of weakness in the face of the Solomon Jesus.[125] See Plate 15 (only a portion of the whole picture is shown here).

Emil Bock points out that there are a number of forerunners to such paintings 'which suggest that in certain painting schools ... a knowledge of the two Jesus children may have continued on'. He mentions, as an example, a Byzantine miniature of the ninth century, an illustration to

De dogmata et constitutione episcoporum by Gregory of Nazianzus,[126] one of the four great Greek doctors of the Church (AD 329–89).

*

The primal wisdom of Ancient Persia, of Zarathustra—the intuitive knowledge of both the starry heavens and the earth—that had come down through the ages and found expression in the wisdom of the Solomon Jesus child 'dies into' or, rather, is metamorphosed through its union with the highest form of angelic innocence, of purest, selfless love and compassion manifest in the Nathan Jesus child. Whereas Buddha sought to free mankind from the fetters of earth-existence, the Christ Being, who descended into the 30-year-old Solomon/Nathan Jesus at the Baptism by John, brought a new, creative meaning to the life of human beings on earth. This was not to free them from physical existence but, through selfless love for the earth and all that 'dwells' on it in unison with reverence and inner, conscious understanding and recognition of the Divine, of the spiritual, creative forces working in and through earth-existence, to cultivate out of the power of free-will (not therefore bound by the ties of blood prevailing before Christ's life and death on earth) 'the principle of love to its highest degree'. In a lecture Rudolf Steiner gave on the Gospel of St John he stated that when the Earth has reached the end of its evolution, love should permeate it through and through (20 May 1908). The 'seed' for this process was 'sown', we could say, in the union of the Zarathustra stream and the Buddha stream in the temple. It lay 'dormant' until Christ's death in the physical body on the Cross and his Resurrection in the spiritual body, when it was given the Water of Life and handed on to humankind to nurture its future growth.

*

We have seen that the idea of two Jesus children, spoken about by Rudolf Steiner as early as 1909, is supported in some of the Christian apocryphal gospels, in Gnostic texts and, above all, in some of the Dead Sea Scrolls first discovered at Qumran. We have also seen that there was present a line of Essene secret teaching which continued within Christian circles and that a tradition of the existence of two Jesus children prevailed in Christian art up to the Renaissance. There is therefore some justification in seriously suggesting an affirmative answer to the question 'Were there two Jesus children?'—the one spoken of in Matthew's Gospel the other in that of Luke.

Notes

1. For a far more detailed exposition see David Ovason, *The Two Children*, and Hella Krause-Zimmer, *Die zwei Jesusknaben in der bildenden Kunst* and *Herod und der Stern von Bethlehem*. See also Emil Bock, *The Childhood of Jesus. The Unknown Years*. Ovason and Krause-Zimmer both consider sculpture as well as paintings in their studies of the existence of two Jesus children.

2. 'The Jewish kingdom was abolished in the external sense along with Jechoniah. Under his rule the people lost their freedom and were led away into the Babylonian exile by Nebuchadnezzar . . . After Jechoniah, during the exile and in the age that followed, there undoubtedly existed an uninterrupted line of uncrowned Jewish kings.' See Emil Bock, *The Childhood of Jesus*, pp. 43–4.

3. It is not easy to determine precisely when the Magi became known as kings, though one Syrian text describes them as Persian priest-kings (*Cave of Treasures*). Matthew is not specific about how many Magi paid homage to the Jesus child, but the fact that they brought three gifts was taken by early commentators to suggest that it was *three* Wise Men who made the long journey to Bethlehem. In the catacombs there are representations of two, three or more Magi.

4. See Emil Bock, *Moses. From the Mysteries of Egypt to the Judges of Israel*, in particular chapter 3.1, pp. 143–8.

5. See *The Times*, 23 October 2002, and www.earlychristianwritings.com/james-bone-box.html

6. *The Festal Menaion* is the book that contains all the services (including the hymns) for the fixed days of celebration for Christ Jesus and his mother—and certain saints.

7. See Emil Bock, *The Childhood of Jesus*, p. 45.

8. Jacobus de Voragine, *Aurea Legenda* or *The Golden Legend*, 'The Nativity of our Lady'.

9. See Bock, *The Childhood of Jesus.*

10. One source of the 'Three Kings' concept is found in Psalm 72:10–11. The Greek word for 'wise men' is *magoi*, which is derived from the Persian word for priest.

11. Regarding the Magi and the Star, see Andrew Welburn, *The Beginnings of Christianity*, pp. 81–6.

12. In *The Childhood of Jesus* Emil Bock refers to a legend that Jacobus de Voragine, Archbishop of Genoa, included in his book *Legenda Aurea* or *The Golden Legend*. This medieval legend traces the shepherds' experience back to their involvement in ancient sun cults. It says that 'twice a year the shepherds held watch over their flocks at night—during the longest and the shortest night of the year. For it was a custom long ago among the heathens that during the two solstices of the sun they held watch over their flocks. This took place in the summer around the time of the festival of John the Baptist and in winter around the time of the birth of the Lord. This they did in honour of the sun which they worshipped.'

13. Valeska Krüger in *The Christian Community Journal*, no. 3, May–June 1970.

14. Ormond Edwards refers here to Emil Schürer's work *The History of the Jewish People in the Age of Jesus Christ* (1973). See also Raymond E. Brown, *The Birth of the Messiah*, pp. 395–6 *et passim.*

15. For a more detailed study, see Ormond Edwards, *The Time of Christ. A Chronology of the Incarnation* (1986), chapter 7; Robert Powell, *Chronicle of the Risen Christ*, chapters 1, 3 and 5; Edward Reaugh Smith, *The Burning Bush*, pp. 82–5.

16. Bock, *The Childhood of Jesus.*

17. From Emil Bock's translation of this Gospel in *The Childhood of Jesus.*

18. Bock, *The Childhood of Jesus.*

19. The New English Bible, New Testament, p. 100.

20. Rudolf Frieling, *Old Testament Studies.*

21. One tradition speaks of a cave or a grotto. Regarding the Star, see R.E. Brown, *The Birth of the Messiah*, p. 36 *et passim*.
22. Moses' brother and the first high priest.
23. See R.E. Brown, p. 441 *et passim*.
24. The name Potiphar or Potiphera signifies 'the priest of the holy bull' (Apis). 'Like all twelve sons of Jacob, Joseph too received his nature and strength from one of the twelve constellations of the Zodiac' (Emil Bock, *Genesis. Creation and the Patriarchs*, p. 167). See also Deuteronomy 33:17.
25. It is an interesting fact that the word Egypt occurs 680 times in the Bible, whereas in Egyptian texts the name of Israel appears once only—on a triumphal stela of the year 5 of Merneptah, the successor of Ramses II (*c.* 1230 BC). See Georges Posner (ed.), *A Dictionary of Egyptian Civilization*.
26. Bock, *The Childhood of Jesus*.
27. The first time that Luke draws our attention to this mystical fact is in chapter 2 where we hear the twelve-year-old boy tell his mother and Joseph that he 'must be about [his] Father's business'.
28. John Baggley, *Doors of Perception—icons and their spiritual significance*, p. 142.
29. Caves were frequently used to house animals.
30. Another well-known example is Rembrandt's *Adoration of the Shepherds*. See Hans Werner Schroeder, *The Cosmic Christ*, pp. 51–2.
31. Active late fifteenth century.
32. *Revelations of St Bridget on the Life and Passion of Our Lord and the Life of His Blessed Mother*.
33. Hall's *Dictionary of Subjects & Symbols in Art*.
34. Washington Gallery of Art.
35. For a detailed description of this complex picture see Ovason, *The Two Children* (2001), pp. 384–8.
36. I am indebted to the Revd Alfred Heidenreich here. See *The Unknown in the Gospels*, lecture 2.
37. Aaron, the elder brother of Moses, was the founder of the Jewish priesthood, the first Jewish High Priest.

38. Rudolf Frieling, *New Testament Studies*, pp. 125–6. See also pp. 152–4 regarding cosmic aspects in Matthew's Gospel.

39. E.R. Smith, *David's Question 'What is Man?'*, p. 103.

40. There is mention of Christ enthroned in the first chapter of Luke's Gospel. However, it is in Matthew's Gospel that our attention is especially drawn to this emblem of royalty. See Matthew 5:34; 19:28; 23:22; 25:31.

41. Early sixth century.

42. See Andrew Welburn, *The Book with Fourteen Seals*, chapter 13.

43. See also Matthew 5:34; 23:22; 25:31; Luke 1:32; 22:30.

44. The Council of Ephesus (431), the third ecumenical council of the Christian Church, was significant for, *inter alia*, its dogmatic decrees on the position of the Virgin Mary in the celestial hierarchy. It was convened by the Eastern Roman Emperor Theodosius II with the approval of Pope Celestine I in order to respond to the teachings of Nestorius that Mary be considered only the 'mother of Christ' and not the 'mother of God'. An accord was reached in which the appellation 'mother of God', formally agreed by the Council, was accepted by all.

45. The scroll may also be interpreted as being a symbol of intelligence and wisdom.

46. See Maria Giovanna Muzl, *Transfiguration. Introduction to the Contemplation of Icons*.

47. Bock, *The Childhood of Jesus*, p. 134; see also Rudolf Steiner, *From Jesus to Christ*, lecture of 12 October, 1911.

48. Today the ceremony of Bar Mitzvah celebrates and confers upon the 13-year-old Jewish male the status of an adult who thenceforth is responsible for his moral and religious duties.

49. On the significance of 'three days' journey' see E.R. Smith (1997), pp. 312–27.

50. Ovason, *The Two Children*.

51. *c.* 1435–95.

52. Concerning the meaning of the term 'the Cosmic Christ', see Hans-Werner Schröder's book of that title.

53. Among the many portrayals of this relationship mention is made here of the depiction of the nativity (shepherds) in *Les tres riches Heures du Duc de Berry*. In the Malvern Priory, in Great Malvern, Worcestershire, there is a stained-glass window depicting the Nathan Jesus in the Temple which shows his true Father, namely God, gazing down upon him. A magnificent mosaic by Pietro Cavallini (fl. 1250–1330) shows us not God the Father but God the Son, the spiritual being of Christ himself, looking down upon Mary at the moment of the Annunciation.

54. *The Gospel of Thomas*, in the Greek text A, given by Tischendorf, translated by Montague Rhodes James, in *The Apocryphal New Testament*.

55. Ibid, p. 54.

56. '[This] document may well come from those Essenes who belonged to the "Community of the Star" near Damascus, rather than having settled in Qumran' (Welburn, 1994, p. 123). However, Charlotte Hampel in her detailed study of the Damascus Texts (see Bibliography) posits that, in all likelihood, two medieval copies of an ancient copy of the Damascus Document, which was part of the Qumran library, reached the Jewish community in Cairo and ended up in the *genizah* (a storeroom attached to a synagogue) where they were recovered, together with other texts, at the end of the ninteeenth century. The Cambridge Talmud scholar Solomon Schechter published the first edition of the Damascus Document in 1910 under the title *Fragments of a Zadokite Work*. Hempel points out that this title was chosen because the community behind parts of the document seems to refer to itself as 'the sons of Zadok'.

57. See Lecture V in the cycle of lectures entitled *The Gospel of St Luke*.

58. A lucid and comprehensive summary of Rudolf Steiner's many statements regarding the two Jesus children—and their respective parents—is given in E.R. Smith's two books *The*

Burning Bush (1997), pp. 33–85 and 313–27, and *The Incredible Births of Jesus* (2001).

59. See Rudolf Steiner, *From Jesus to Christ*, ten lectures given in Karlsruhe, 5–14 October 1911, especially Lecture VIII; *The Spiritual Guidance of the Individual and Humanity*, Lecture III; and *The Gospel of St Matthew*, Lectures V and VI. See also Pietro Archiati, *The Great Religions*, chapter 3.

60. Of Worcester Cathedral.

61. R. Steiner, Lectures 2, 4, 6 and 7. Elsewhere: 'He had been incarnated again and again; lastly during the Babylonian-Chaldaic civilization, and now as the Solomon Jesus-child', *From Jesus to Christ*, Lecture VIII, 12 October 1911.

62. See *Die Brücke zwischen der Weltgeistigkeit und dem Physischen des Menschen*, a series of 16 lectures given by Rudolf Steiner, 26 November–23 December 1920. Not yet published in English.

63. In his book *The Childhood of Jesus* Emil Bock makes the point that this inner connection remained alive until the Middle Ages and has often been expressed in words, especially by theologians of Syrian and Armenian Christendom. According to Steiner the Zarathustra referred to here was one of the incarnations of Zarathustra the Prophet of the sixth or seventh millennium BC.

64. See *The Nag Hammadi Library* (ed. James M. Robinson), E.J. Brill, Leiden 1977, pp. 256–64.

65. A star was symbolic of a god or a deified king, in the ancient Middle East—stars appear on carved signature seals and wall-carvings.

66. This rendering is to be found in Robin Alexander's translation of Georg Blattmann's book *Die Sonne—Gestirn und Gottheit*. See Bibliography: English title *The Sun. The Ancient Mysteries and New Physics*.

67. See Jakob Streit, *Sun and Cross*, Floris Books, Edinburgh (2004), p. 30.

68. On Zarathustra's reincarnations, see Welburn, *The Beginnings of Christianity* (1991), chapter 3, p. 44.

69. G. Ashe, *The Ancient Wisdom* (Macmillan 1977).
70. See also Paul's Epistle to the Colossians 1:17.
71. See Barbara Watterson, *Gods of Ancient Egypt*.
72. The cult of Mithras (the Persian god of light and the sun) spread from Persia through the Roman Empire from the second half of the first century BC. It became a serious rival to Christianity, but declined in the fourth century AD.

    In AD 313 the Emperor Constantine accorded to Christianity the rights and toleration previously enjoyed by paganism, and in AD 380 the Roman Emperor Theodosius I established it as the one and only state religion.
73. See, for instance, R. Steiner, *The Gospel of St John and its relation to the other Gospels*, Lecture I, 24 June 1909; *The Influence of Spiritual Beings upon Man*, Lecture VI, 24 March 1908; *The Book of Revelation and the work of the priest*, Lecture VIII, 12 September 1924.
74. AD 354–430.
75. R. Steiner, the opening lecture dated 4 October 1911 of a series entitled *From Jesus to Christ*.
76. See Bibliography.
77. R. Steiner, lecture entitled 'The Need for Christ', 5 January 1923. In the Journal *Anthroposophical Quarterly*, vol. 15, no. 3, 1970.
78. For the variety of sun symbols, see Streit, *Sun and Cross*.
79. See Miranda Green, regarding the pre-Christian cult of the sun.
80. See *The Dictionary of the Liturgy* by the Revd Jovian P. Lang, OFM (Catholic Book Publishing Co., New York 1989), p. 436.
81. See note 66.
82. According to the apocryphal *Book of James*. Jacobus de Voragine, 1230–98, Archbishop of Genoa, in *Aurea Legenda* or *Golden Legend* (published about 1275), recounts this too (translated by William Caxton into English in 1483). All suitors for the hand of Mary were to bring rods to be placed

on the altar of the temple. It had been prophesized that the rod which burst into flower and on which a dove should rest would indicate the suitor who would win the hand of the virgin. It was the rod placed by Joseph which was 'blessed' by the presence of the dove. Several stages of this rod ritual were portrayed by Giotto in the Scrovegni Chapel, Padua. The process of breaking the rod in half by the disappointed suitors is magnificently depicted by Perugino and Raphael.

83. Rudolf Steiner, *The Gospel of St Luke*, lecture of 19 September 1909.
84. Ovason, p. 159.
85. Luke 2:40.
86. See note 83.
87. In R. Steiner, *The Festivals and their Meaning*, lecture given on 1 January 1921.
88. See www.skidmore.edu/-m_mcgort/history.html. Today Nazareth is the largest Arab city in Israel with a population of about 60,000, half Christians, half Moslems.
89. For further details see J.D. Crossan and J.L. Reed, *Excavating Jesus*, pp. 33–5.
90. Nazareth received no mention by any contemporary historian. It is not mentioned in the Old Testament, the Talmud (the Jewish law book), nor in the Apocrypha, and it finds no mention in any rabbinic literature. Nazareth was not included in the list of settlements of the tribes of Zebulon (*Joshua* 19:10–16) which mentions twelve towns and six villages, nor is it included among the 45 cities of Galilee that were mentioned by Flavius Josephus (Jewish historian, AD 37–*c*. 100).
91. Justin Martyr, *c*. 100–*c*. 165, was the most important Christian 'apologist' of the second century.
92. Bock, *The Childhood of Jesus*, chapter XI. See also the discussion that took place on 21 April 1923 between Rudolf Steiner and the workers at the first Goetheanum, Switzerland. Published in the collection of similar discussions under the title *From Limestone to Lucifer* (Rudolf Steiner Press, 1999).

93. See Ormond Edwards, *A New Chronology of the Gospels*, p. 39. Raymond E. Brown considers quite different dates, see pp. 166–7 *et passim*. So, too, does Robert Powell, see Bibliography. See also Edward Reaugh Smith, pp. 82–5.

94. The New English Bible, New Testament.

95. See also Matthew 3:16–17; Mark 1:10–11; John 1:32–3.

96. Steiner gives us a closer understanding of the meaning of the phrase 'the inward became outward' in Lecture VI (6 September 1910) of the cycle *The Gospel of St Matthew*.

97. Bock, *The Childhood of Jesus*, pp. 89–90.

98. Andrew Welburn, *The Beginnings of Christianity. Essene mystery, Gnostic revelation and the Christian vision*, p. 135.

99. A pre-Christian, Jewish mystical sect. See Andrew Welburn, *Gnosis. The Mysteries and Christianity*.

100. 'Messiah' is the Hebrew word *mashiah*, which can also be translated 'anointed one'.

101. At what stage Essenic dual Messianism arose is not known, but it was probably in the Hasmonean period (166–63 BC) that sacerdotal Messianism coalesced with the traditional Davidic promise. See Ormond Edwards, *The Time of Christ*, p. 50.

102. The Levites were distributed around the tabernacle, nearer the holy place than the eleven other tribes (see Numbers 2).

103. Geza Vermes, *The Complete Dead Sea Scrolls in English*, p. 110.

104. See Ovason, p. 137. He makes the point that these references were expurgated by certain scholars who, not knowing what to make of a plurality of 'Messiahs', dropped the plural endings.

105. Published in 1955 by D. Barthélemy in *Qumran Cave 1* (Oxford), pp. 107–18.

106. See I Chronicles 12:27.

107. Not to be confused with Simeon we hear about in Luke's Gospel.

108. See: www.voiceoffaith.com/simeon.html

109. See: www.voiceoffaith.com/judah.html

110. An embroidered vestment worn by ancient Hebrew priests.

111. Purple was formerly worn as a symbol of royalty.
112. See G. Vermes, pp. 247–9.
113. *The Beginnings of Christianity*, p. 129.
114. Ibid., p. 130. See also Welburn's note (no. 9) on page 319.
115. AD *c*. 339–397. Ambrose is numbered among the four great Latin doctors of the Church, with Augustine, Jerome and Gregory the Great.
116. Karl Georg Kuhn, 'The Two Messiahs of Aaron and Israel' in *The Scrolls of the New Testament* (ed. K. Stendahl). See also Ovason, p. 137.
117. In her book *Die Zwei Jesusknaben*, Krause-Zimmer discusses over 30 works of art which show the presence of two Jesus children. Ovason claims to have identified a further 100 or so paintings. He makes the interesting point that they were all the works of Italian artists, and completed within less than half a century of each other. These facts, he says, speak for themselves: 'the theme of the two children was developed by artists in Italy, probably starting in Venice and reaching Florence soon afterwards'.
118. Mark's Gospel 1:6.
119. Regarding the spelling *Angius* see Ovason, p. 287.
120. Bock, *The Childhood of Jesus*, p. 83.
121. See also Acts 1:14.
122. Ambrogio Bergognone was born in the city he was named after. His real name was Ambrogio da Fossano.
123. In the Museo dell'Opera del Duomo, Siena.
124. R. Steiner, Lecture 10 in *From Limestone to Lucifer*, 21 April 1923; also *The Gospel of St Luke*, Lecture 7, 21 September 1909.
125. See Ovason, p. 189.
126. Bibliothèque nationale, Ms.gr.510 fol. 165, Paris. See Emil Bock, *The Childhood of Jesus*, p. 84.

Bibliography

The Bible. Authorized Version
The New English Bible. New Testament
The Apocryphal New Testament

*

Allegro, John, *The Dead Sea Scrolls* (Penguin Books, 1974)
Baggley, John, *Doors of Perception—Icons and their spiritual significance* (Mowbray, London and Oxford 1987)
Bittleston, Adam, *Our Spiritual Companions* (Floris Books, Edinburgh 1980)
—*Human Needs and Cosmic Answers. The Spirit of the Circling Stars* (Floris Books, Edinburgh 1993)
Blattmann, Georg, *The Sun. The Ancient Mysteries and a New Physics* (Floris Books, Edinburgh 1985). Translation by Robin Alexander of *Die Sonne—Gestirn und Gottheit* (Verlag Urachhaus, Stuttgart 1972)
Bock, Emil, *Genesis. Creation and the Patriarchs* (Floris Books, Edinburgh 1983)
—*Moses. From the Mysteries of Egypt to the Judges of Israel* (Floris Books, Edinburgh 1986)
—*The Childhood of Jesus. The Unknown Years* (Floris Books, Edinburgh 1997)
—*Caesars and Apostles* (Floris Books, Edinburgh 1998)
—*Saint Paul. Life, Epistles and Teaching* (Floris Books, Edinburgh 1993)
—*Threefold Mary* (Anthroposophic Press, Great Barrington 2003)
Brown, Raymond E., *Birth of the Messiah* (Doubleday Books 1999)
Collins, J.J., *The Sceptre and the Star: The Messiahs of the Dead Sea Scrolls and Other Ancient Literature* (Doubleday, New York 1995)

Crossan, John Dominic & Jonathan L. Reed, *Excavating Jesus. Beneath the Stones, Behind the Texts* (SPCK 2001)

Edwards, Ormond, *A New Chronology of the Gospels* (Floris Books, Edinburgh 1972)

—*The Time of Christ. A Chronology of the Incarnation* (Floris Books 1986)

Ferrura, Antonio, *Katakomben. Unbekannte Bilder des frühen Christentums unter der Via Latina* (Verlag Urachhaus, Stuttgart 1991)

Frieling, Rudolf, *Old Testament Studies* (Floris Books, Edinburgh 1987)

—*Studies in the New Testament* (Floris Books, Edinburgh 1994)

Gettings, Fred, *The Hidden Art. A study of occult symbolism* (Studio Vista, 1978)

Green, Miranda, *The Sun-Gods of Ancient Europe* (B.T. Batsford, London 1991)

Hawkes, Jacquetta, *Man and the Sun* (The Cresset Press, London 1962)

Heidenreich, Alfred, *The Unknown in the Gospels* (Christian Community Press, London 1972)

Hempel, Charlotte, *The Damascus Texts* (Sheffield Academic Press, 2000)

Hiebel, Frederick, *Treasures of Biblical Research and the Conscience of the Times* (Anthroposophic Press, New York 1970)

James, Montague Rhodes (tr.), *The Apocryphal New Testament* (Oxford University Press)

Krause-Zimmer, Hella, *Echnaton. König im Frühlicht der Zeitenwende* (Verlag Walter Keller, Dornach 1972)

—*Die Zwei Jesusknaben in der bildenden Kunst* (Freies Geistesleben, Stuttgart 1986)

—*Herod und der Stern von Bethlehem* (Freies Gestesleben, Stuttgart 1997)

Kuhn, Karl Georg, 'The Two Messiahs of Aaron and Israel' in *The Scrolls of the New Testament*, Stendahl, K. (ed.) (SCM, London 1958)

Muzl, Maria Giovanna, *Transfiguration. Introduction to the Contemplation of Icons* (St Paul Media Productions, UK n.d.)

Ovason, David, *The Two Children* (Century, London 2001)

Posner, Georges (ed.), *A Dictionary of Egyptian Civilization* (Methuen, London 1962)

Powell, Robert, *Chronicle of the Living Christ* (Anthroposophic Press, New York 1996)

Schechter, Solomon, *Documents of Jewish Sectaries. I. Fragments of a Zadokite Work* (Cambridge University Press, 1910)

Schroeder, Hans Werner, *The Cosmic Christ* (Floris Books, Edinburgh 1997)

Shepherd, A.P., *A Scientist of the Invisible* (Hodder and Stoughton, London 1975)

Smith, Edward Reaugh, *The Burning Bush. Rudolf Steiner, Anthroposophy and the Holy Scriptures* (Anthroposophic Press, New York 1997)

—*The Incredible Birth of Jesus* (Anthroposophic Press, New York 1998)

—*David's Question 'What is Man?'* (Anthroposophic Press, New York 2001)

Steiner, Rudolf, *Christianity as Mystical Fact* (Rudolf Steiner Press, London 1972) chapter VI, 'Egyptian Mystery Wisdom'.

—*The Festivals and their Meaning* (Rudolf Steiner Press, London 1981), lectures of 27 December 1914 and 1 January 1921

—*The Fifth Gospel* (Rudolf Steiner Press, London 1995), Lectures VII and XII, 4 November 1913 and 17 December 1913

—*From Jesus to Christ* (Rudolf Steiner Press, 1991), Lectures I and VIII, 4 October 1911 and 12 October 1911

—*The Gospel of St John and its relation to the other three Gospels* (Anthroposophic Press, New York 1982), Lecture I, 24 June 1909

—*Gospel of St Luke* (Rudolf Steiner Press, London, 1975), Lectures V and VII, 19 September 1909 and 21 September 1909

—*Gospel of St Matthew* (Rudolf Steiner Press, London 1965), Lecture VI, 6 September 1910

—*The Occult Significance of the Bhagavad Gita* (Anthroposophic Press, New York 1968), Lecture IV, 31 May 1913

—*The Search for the New Isis the Divine Sophia* (Mercury Press, New York 1983)

—*The Spiritual Guidance of the Individual and Humanity* (Anthroposophic Press, New York 1992, Lecture III, 8 June 1911)

Streit, Jakob, *Sun and Cross* (Floris Books, Edinburgh 2004)

Vermes, Geza, *The Dead Sea Scrolls* (Cleveland, Ohio, 1978)

Voragine, Jacobus de, *The Golden Legend* (numerous editions in several European languages)

Ware, Archimandrite Kallistos & Mother Mary (trs.), *The Festal Menaion* (Faber & Faber, 1969)

Watterson, Barbara, *Gods of Ancient Egypt* (Sutton Publishing Ltd, Stroud, Glos., 1996)

Weitzmann, K. (et al.), *The Icon* (Bracken Books, London 1982)

Welburn, Andrew, *The Beginnings of Christianity. Essene mystery, Gnostic revelation and the Christian vision* (Floris Books, Edinburgh 1991)

—*The Book with Fourteen Seals* (Rudolf Steiner Press, Sussex 1991)

—*Gnosis. The Mysteries and Christianity* (Floris Books, Edinburgh 1994)

Wallis Budge, E.A., *The Book of the Dead* (Routledge & Kegan Paul, London 1949)

Michael and the Two-Horned Beast
The Challenge of Evil Today in the Light of Rudolf Steiner's Science of the Spirit

Bernard Nesfield-Cookson

In our materialistic and sceptical age, some people find it difficult to take seriously the existence of real spiritual beings. Nevertheless, countless individuals—from the historic founders of religions to those who have been through near-death experiences—have confirmed the reality of such entities from their direct personal experience. Such people have spoken of beings of Light, such as Angels and Archangels, and 'evil' beings, spirits of darkness.

From his own seership, Rudolf Steiner described the varied forces of evil in our time, and their principal opponent, the Archangel Michael. Basing his work on Steiner's teachings, the author presents an epic picture of forces of 'good' and 'evil'—a battle of cosmic dimensions in which we are all intimately involved. He clarifies the pivotal role of the Archangel Michael, the 'Guardian of Cosmic Intelligence', who fights to hold the balance between the key powers of evil in our time, Lucifer and Ahriman, and describes other members of the evil hierarchies, the Sun Demon and the Asuras. He also discusses the biblical Apocalypse of St John, the Mexican Mysteries, the Knights Templars, the physical incarnation on earth of Ahriman, the Eighth Sphere, the human 'Double', and much else.

This book is an essential guide to meeting the challenge of evil at the new millennium, and strengthening the forces of Light.

384pp; 21.5 × 13.5 cm; paperback; £16.95; ISBN 0 904693 98 8

Timothy
   2:15-18

MATTHEW - 24.2
          24.3
          24.30 →

ROMANS - 8:11

MATTHEW - 24.21

DISTRUCTION JERUSALEM

   AD 70

SODOM-GOMARRH-

FLOOD   WWI WWII

JEWS HOLCUS